Americosis

AMERICOSIS

A Nation's Dysfunction Observed from Public Transit

SAM FORSTER

Toronto, 2023

Sutherland House
416 Moore Ave., Suite 205
Toronto, ON M4G 1C9

First edition, October 2023

If you are interested in inviting one of our authors to a live event or media appearance, please contact sranasinghe@sutherlandhousebooks.com and visit our website at sutherlandhousebooks.com for more information about our authors and their schedules.

We acknowledge the support of the Government of Canada.

Manufactured in China
Cover designed by Lena Yang and Jordan Lunn

Library and Archives Canada Cataloguing in Publication
Title: Americosis : a nation's dysfunction observed from public transit / Samuel Forster.
Names: Forster, Samuel (Freelance writer), author.
Identifiers: Canadiana (print) 20230457762 | Canadiana (ebook) 20230457789 | ISBN 9781990823282 (softcover) | ISBN 9781990823404 (EPUB)
Subjects: LCSH: United States–Social conditions–2020- | LCSH: Local transit–United States.
Classification: LCC HN59.3 .F67 2023 | DDC 306.097309/052–dc23

ISBN 978-1-990823-28-2
eBook 978-1-990823-40-4

To Carl, the stoic, still above ground with no complaints.

And to the toothless vagrant who offered to blow me for a pack of Swisher Sweets at Pacific and Lamar; I hope you find peace in this world.

TABLE OF CONTENTS

AUTHOR'S NOTE

VIRTUALLY ALL OF THE PROBLEMS with the modern American mode of living stem from three major cultural characteristics: a pathological attachment to the automobile, a horrifying apathy toward the obesity epidemic, and a deeply engrained fetishization of employment. This should already be plain to anyone paying attention, but it's especially clear if you sell your car and spend six grueling months riding public transit in Dallas, Texas, arguably the nation's most regrettable example of urban dysfunction.

For half a year, I got on the train in one of the biggest cities in the wealthiest nation of all time only to find myself surrounded by people who are either homeless or commuting to a job that hardly keeps them above the poverty line. Most of them are morbidly obese, and those who aren't are mostly slim because of heroin or some other destructive analgesic. This country is in shambles for reasons that are material and obvious, but if you turn on the TV, the only issues our political and media intelligentsia find time to talk about are drag queens, QAnon crackpots, the sexual misadventures of partisan pseudo-celebrities, and other sparkly hysterias. It's ludicrous political stagecraft that has absolutely nothing to do with the lives of normal Americans, to say nothing of the weakest and most miserable.

These conditions, which constitute a clear cultural disease, are so ugly and glaring that a diagnostic report like this really shouldn't be necessary.

Alas, here it is.

Up front, I feel compelled to make a brief note about race. Dallas has a long, thorny, and at times very dark racial history—as do Texas and the United States more broadly. I could have written a very lengthy, very detailed book about all of the horrific ways in which this city, this state, and this country have treated their minorities in the past and about all of the ways in which those historic wounds continue to fester. That's not what this book is about.

Still, I've received feedback suggesting that a note about rider demographics would provide useful context. According to official stats, 51 percent of DART riders are Black, 20 percent are Latino, 19 percent are white, and 10 percent are mixed race.[1] My experience is that those figures dramatically overestimate how many white people ride DART. Frequently, I would get on a train or bus with dozens of other people, and I would be the only white person. There was one day where I rode nearly the entire length of the Green Line without seeing another white person. Again, there's a whole book that could be written about why that is, but this isn't it.

PREFACE

WHO GAINS FROM SCARCITY AS well as from abundance? Who benefits magnificently from the greatest disasters? Who seizes all the favorable positions, strategic posts, and bases of operation in commerce and industry? Who invades all and becomes master of all, but the big speculators and banks, and, in every industry, the big Capitals?

Yes, it is time for the middle classes, already seriously encroached upon, to watch out. Money invades all; the power of the big Capitals relentlessly increases. They attract and absorb, in all domains, the small capitals and the middle-sized fortunes.

Thus, despite the theoretically democratic principle of economic freedom, or rather, because of this freedom, which is false and illusory like all simple and unorganized freedoms, capitals press on other capitals without counterweight and in proportion to their mass, becoming concentrated in the hands of the largest holders. Society tends to be divided more and more sharply into two major classes: an elite owning all or nearly all, absolute master in the realms of landed property, commerce, and industry; and the masses owning nothing, living in total collective dependence on the owners of capital and instruments of production, and who, for a precarious and always decreasing wage, are forced to rent their arms, talents, and strength to the Feudal Lords of modern Society.

— Victor Prosper Considerant, Manifesto of Democracy (1847)

Yeah.

Looking out at the Dallas skyline, a cluster of modernist skyscrapers that house America's most dominant institutions, I'm tempted to believe Considerant wasted his time with this place. Surely, he would be impressed to learn that the site of his utopian colony would one day be occupied by a metropolis wealthier than Munich, Mumbai, Madrid, or Moscow, but Dallas clearly bears no resemblance to what he had envisioned.

The foremost disciple of French proto-socialist Charles Fourier, Considerant was a strident advocate for liberalization and reform throughout the decade leading up to the French Revolution of 1848. He published his 1847 magnum opus just months before the release of Marx's revolutionary *Communist Manifesto*. Like very few of his contemporaries, Considerant envisioned an economic system that furthered the cause of the common man in the same way it did the propertied aristocrats.

As a consequence of his political agitation against the military exploits and domestic tyranny of Louis Napoleon Bonaparte, he was forced into exile in Belgium, where he eventually connected with American Fourierists intent on colonizing Texas, a jurisdiction that had just recently swapped sovereignty for statehood. In 1855, a year before the formal incorporation of Dallas, Considerant purchased 2,500 acres on the south bank of the Trinity and recruited a few hundred colonists who were eager to escape the anguish and drudgery of French proletarianism. This new colony, La Reunion, was intended to be a place where decisions followed direct democracy and where respect for individual property rights would be balanced by the promise of generous communal redistribution—a radical contrast to the bleak socioeconomic reality of nineteenth-century France.

Alas, La Reunion would be a short-lived project. Owing to an unusually cruel winter in 1856, the denizens of the emergent community found themselves unable to maintain their agricultural operations at anything approaching sufficiency. A financial death spiral ensued, morale plummeted, and, by 1859, the colony was abandoned. The area would soon be subsumed by its rapidly expanding, ideologically aimless counterpart: Dallas. Today, La Reunion lives on as the namesake of Dallas's most recognizable tower, as one of the ugliest downtown neighborhoods in the country, as a fun bit of local trivia, and absolutely nothing more. A century and a half later, it's almost uncanny how different Dallas is from the socialist paradise imagined by Considerant and his hopeful coterie.

Like Considerant, I came to North Texas as a transplant from the Francosphere, having lived in Montreal up until the summer of 2020. The reasons for my move aren't all that important, but the fact of the matter is that writing this book would not have occurred to me had my introduction to Dallas not been preceded by life in North America's nicest city. The beautiful parks, beautiful markets, beautiful people, and beautiful impressions of community in Montreal are truly striking and without parallel on the continent. Like all places, it has its drawbacks and imperfections, but there's a certain feeling of joy and vitality one gets—the experience of a natural existence, or at least a base contentment that the physical world around you is not conspiring to make life hellish. Simply put, Montreal is livable.

Dallas is decidedly unlivable. It is functionally and aesthetically antithetical to Montreal, and over the course of the past six months, I've walked its streets, rode its transit, and immersed myself among its most beleaguered losers to learn why. The reasons are clear, and the longer I live here, the more I realize that you actually don't need to be particularly observant or insightful to figure out why things in America are as fucked up as they are. You don't need to be an academic anthropologist or a trained statistician. You just need to be in the mix, on the ground. If you go out into the real world and stroll around, it will become rather plain that three factors account for almost all of the misery in this city and, more broadly, in this country.

First, the cultural centrality of the automobile has completely mutilated the urban form. It has drained public and private coffers alike, and it has caused atomization that precludes the sort of interclass cohesion required for a healthy society. American car culture is pathologically destructive, and nowhere is that effect more visible than in Dallas. Unlike New York, Chicago, or DC, no one making above $25,000 a year rides public transit in Dallas. Among major American cities and, indeed, among major global cities, the modal share for public transportation is by far the worst in Dallas. This is to say that there is no city in the world as large as Dallas where fewer people elect to travel aboard trains and buses, shoulder-to-shoulder with their fellow man. Consequently, nobody with social or political capital has any firsthand experience with or any concern for the permanent underclass that is the ridership of Dallas Area Rapid Transit (DART).

Second, virtually everyone that lives here is either overweight or obese, a reality that is ceaselessly and ruthlessly perpetuated by a state-subsidized food complex that actively infuses everything we eat with poison. It's truly appalling how little media attention this crisis receives. Far more Americans died this year of obesity-related illnesses than from COVID-19, and of the country's top ten largest metropolitan statistical areas, Dallas-Fort Worth stands alone as the fattest.

Third, there are many people who have jobs that are unproductive and often even counterproductive because of America's cultural fetishization of "employment" and its cultural aversion to basic redistributive social policies. In the Lone Star State, home of the fiercely individualistic cowboy capitalist, oligarchs enjoy cushy corporate handouts while millions mow lawns, stock shelves, and flip burgers for $7.25 an hour. There's this perception that having a job is inherently good or noble, that unemployment is a critical economic statistic, and that there will always be productive work for those who want it. You need only spend a few minutes on a DART train, bus, or downtown sidewalk, face-to-face with the countless members of the permanent underclass, those with no marketable skills or discernible economic future, to be disabused of this outrageous idea. Automation is swiftly plunging these people into an abiding state of precarity and economic obsolescence.

In these ways, Dallas is an exposition of the country's most wounding cultural and economic foibles. For all the vulgarities of late American capitalism and neoliberal excess, Dallas is especially guilty. These problems all exist on a national scale, of course, but the City of Hate is so archetypally American as to teeter on the edge of caricature, as if a room of sniffy Belgian progressives were asked to conjure a *normal* American city from scratch.

Why do people not talk about this stuff? Why do people not care about this stuff? It's so obvious what's going on. It's so obvious how bad everything is. It's absurd that no one has made a political career out of fixating on these glaring issues. Even the pretense of concern should be enough to bring a 538-vote electoral college victory, yet the most desperate issues in the nation are almost never brought up at presidential debates or on the nightly news: car culture has ruined this country; the obesity epidemic has ruined this country; the unflinching normalization of subsistence wage slavery has ruined this country. These are the problems that matter, and they're not at all inconspicuous.

We're all suckers for clickbait, and we all have visceral sensibilities. I get it. I understand this country's endless fascination with the frivolous Culture War issues that preoccupy people, like Hannity, Maddow, and the tens of millions who comprise their respective viewerships. But the phenomena that drive the Culture War, spotlit by our institutions in a shamefully pornographic manner, are miniscule in their impact. Maybe the issues are worth contemplating, but they are certainly not the proximal reason why large swaths of Americans lead such unbearably wretched lives.

On the trains, buses, and ugly, muggy sidewalks of Dallas, it's all so painfully obvious.

CHAPTER 1

Purell Mimosas

ONE THING THAT CANADIANS TEND to find remarkable when they first enter an American grocery store is the vast selection of alcohol. Even after living here for a year, there's still something that seems faintly misplaced about passing a flat of Pepsi-priced Bud Light on your way to the produce section. It still seems decadent and unnatural in a way that's difficult to rationalize or articulate. Perhaps some of my countrymen will know what I mean. Buying alcohol in Canada isn't necessarily hard, but it usually requires a trip to a designated store, one that only admits adults and precocious minors with passable fakes. Picking up alcohol is a distinct outing that requires conscious planning; it's not a task that can just blend in with the tedium of pumping gas or buying laundry detergent. In some provinces, retail activity involving alcoholic beverages must be conducted by crown corporations, bodies that enjoy a near monopoly over sales and distribution. New Brunswickers, for example, buy from the New Brunswick Liquor Corporation, Ontarians from the Liquor Control Board of Ontario, and so on. As one can imagine, this has led to a stale market, a reality that is exacerbated by lofty sin taxes and regulations. There are some exceptions, but booze tends to be much more expensive and out of the way in Canada than in the United States.

At any gas station or grocery store in America, conversely, people can trade pocket change for party-sized containers of nearly every alcohol imaginable. Your buck gets a lot of bang south of the 49th. If for some inexplicable reason you wanted a forty of Olde English, it's $2.99 at 7-Eleven. A tall boy of King Cobra at Target is $2.89. A bottle of Colt 45 from Texaco is $3.49. To each their own. Frankly, all of these options seem heavenly compared to the crude beverage being prepared before me on a brisk November morning on Fitzhugh Avenue, my first day as a real, salt-of-the-earth commuter aboard DART.

I had just arrived at a bus shelter and found myself standing a few paces away from a tired, sullen-looking man in a tattered Cowboys hoodie and sweatpants that looked as though they had never been washed. Although the bus I was expecting ran three times an hour, the man looked like he had been there for days or at least through the night. It was still quite dark, but the streetlamps cast enough light into the shelter for me to see that he was mixing something on his lap. It was something wild. In his right hand was a small container of hand sanitizer, and in his left was a partially filled bottle of Sunny D, the orange drink. Apparently, they still make Sunny D. As casually as if he were adding milk to his coffee, the man poured six or seven ounces of Purell into the Sunny D, tossed the empty container on the ground, and took a long, audacious swig.

There was no struggle—no coughing, wheezing, or wincing like there would have been for the average person. He looked composed and surprisingly nonchalant. It seemed as though he had no paranoia, nor felt any urge to conduct himself discreetly. He was frowning slightly, breathing just loud enough to be audible, and occasionally it appeared that he was mouthing out words, but he wasn't having any trouble keeping the fluid down.

As he sat there, grumbling to himself and periodically lifting the bottle to his lips, I considered all of the different vendors within walking distance that could have sold him something else—something nominally intended for human consumption. Even at six o'clock on a Monday morning, as it was at present, there must have been dozens of places that would have sold him real drinks, like the malt liquors mentioned above, for the price of a cheap coffee.

Maybe the man's austerity wasn't as crazy as it seemed. I stood there quietly and wondered to myself whether the recipe made sense on economic grounds, setting aside all the obvious repercussions of ingesting hand sanitizer. What's the alcohol proof of Purell? 120? 150? Sunny D must cost next to nothing—corn syrup and orange food coloring, essentially. I couldn't see it being more expensive than bottled water. And the hand sanitizer. A few dollars perhaps? Surely less than a cheap Mickey.

He burped, and suddenly the expression on his face changed from one of indignance to amusement. Then he turned and looked at me. Up until this point, I had been observing him out of the corner of my eye, but his direct attention prompted me to stare down toward my phone, as if his antics were infinitely less interesting than the tweets I was pretending to read.

He continued gazing at me, and then he chuckled. It wasn't maniacal laughter or anything unhinged, but the obscurity of it put me on edge.

I managed to keep up the charade of ignoring him for another minute or so, but then something truly foul happened. A small puddle was forming at the man's feet. The whizzing of engines on a nearby freeway was more than enough to mask the sound of trickling, but there was soon enough liquid for me to be certain the man was pissing himself. Like a mop just pulled from a bucket, the right leg of the man's thick cotton pants was fully saturated and releasing a steady drizzle from the cuff.

"You like this shit?" he asked, chuckling and raising the drink toward me.

I turned to him and looked at the bottle. "That's quite the beverage," I replied, trying my best to disregard the pool that was now inching toward my feet.

"Fuck yeah. You wanna try this shit?"

"Uhhh, no. I'm good, thanks."

He looked surprised, eyes widened and neck tilted slightly. "Man, fuck you, man. I tell ya', this shit is mad good, man. MAD-FUCKING-GOOD!"

Why was I even having this conversation? Why didn't I have my car? The sensible thing would be to drive, but that was no longer an option. I had positioned myself among the non-driving class of Dallasites. For better or worse, I had gotten rid of my car to learn about the texture of the city, to see what was going on, and to become a more authentic, engaged metropolitan, or something frivolous like that.

Luckily, the bus arrived, and our uncomfortable interaction came to an end. I got on. He did not. Apparently, he was going to stay put and finish his punchy little elixir. Maybe he'd catch the next one. Maybe he wouldn't.

I do wonder how he spent the remainder of that day.

CHAPTER 2

All Aboard to Nowhere

THE LEXICON OF SOCIAL SCIENCE is filled with hundreds of words that lack any sort of clear or compelling definition, but "homelessness" has to be among the most superficial. The *Oxford English Dictionary* says it's when a person is "without a home, and therefore typically living on the streets." That's more cogent than what gets conjured by the turtlenecks at meetings of the American Sociological Association, so I'll run with it.

However, this definition, too, has its problems. It is actually quite hard to determine who is without a home and who is truly *living* on the streets. Conversely, it is quite obvious that some people do have homes and are therefore definitively not homeless. Jeff Bezos, for example, has the $165 million Warner Estate, among many other extravagant properties. Tiger Woods owns a castle with a small golf course in the backyard. These are men who fit quite cleanly into the non-homeless set of people—those who are not living on the streets. And even at social strata far below them, say that of average CEOs or average professional athletes, it is easy to classify many people as existing firmly among the homed. With pensions and paid-off, four-car-garage manors in affluent suburbs, it's tough to see this demographic ever being in want of basic housing and consumer staples. But as soon as you start to analyze the lives of typical working people, the classification becomes fraught with ambiguity and tenuous economic assumptions. Consider the lives of two Dallasites: Trevor Tramp and Willy Wageslave.

Trevor is extremely poor. He's the sort of person who springs to mind when most people hear the word "homeless." He is unemployed, has obliterated his credit score, pawned all of his personal effects, and now lives transiently. Most nights are spent in public shelters and, when he's lucky, on the sofas of begrudging acquaintances. When he isn't so lucky, it's a park bench or a ventilation grate. If a trip around the world cost a dollar, Trevor couldn't make it to Oklahoma.

Willy is also poor, but at least he has a job at a neighborhood supermarket where he takes home around $1,100 per month. Of that, let's say $250 goes toward food, $150 toward utilities, and $200 toward other miscellaneous expenses like toiletries, clothes, medical bills, and haircuts. If he has no dependents, no car, no outstanding debts, if he puts nothing into savings and spends no money on alcohol, cigarettes, lottery tickets, or any other form of entertainment, then Willy, a man who works forty hours per week, would be able to allocate around $500 per month toward rent.

Now, Dallas is one of the cheapest major cities in the country, but $500 really only goes so far. You'd probably be able to find something nicer than a homeless shelter, but not by much. A cheap motel, maybe, or a shared apartment, or a dingy studio on an unsafe street. And while this income falls well below the threshold for Section 8 assistance, lottery-selected waitlists can take months or even years.

Is Willy better off than Trevor? Is he enjoying a standard of living that is appreciably higher? On paper, it may be tempting to say that he is. Willy has more money, and many people would say that he does in fact have a home. But there is a sort of qualitative despair that equalizes their condition, because if Willy is even the least bit complacent with his finances, he will soon find himself in the exact same position as Trevor. And even if he runs an incredibly tight ship, an unexpected bill of any real significance will very likely force him underwater, breathlessly spiraling into debt at a rate that makes his current lifestyle, modest as it may be, wholly unsustainable. In many ways, the two men lead lives that are more similar than they are different, incessantly strangled by pressures that make escaping the bottom economic quintile virtually impossible.

Maybe Trevor has it better. At least society doesn't waste time holding up pretenses about people like him. There is no cloying illusion that he is anything other than what he is: a broken, utterly ruined man, toiling among a broken, utterly ruined bunch of beggars and misfits. There is no veneer or social mythology impressed upon him as a valued, ascendant member of the workforce. Nor, subsequently, is there any convincing way for society to accept his condition as just or acceptable. Neither Trevor nor Willy have much in the way of material possessions or long-term financial prospects, but at least Trevor owns his time and benefits from a basic cultural consensus that he deserves support. He doesn't have to slog through long days of scanning apples, mopping floors, and endless hours of other easily automated labor just for the privilege of meeting his basic material needs. There is a financial cost to existence that only one of these men is forced to settle for, and it isn't Trevor.

All of this is to say that the economic distinctions between the Trevors and Willys of the world, insofar as such distinctions exist, are a matter of degree and not of kind. And therefore *homelessness*, the way it tends to be defined, lacks the conceptual clarity that would make it a useful metric of socioeconomic health.

The plight of Trevor Tramp is more obvious. Visually, it is easy to distinguish someone who panhandles and sleeps rough from someone who works a menial service job. There is something uniquely disruptive and objectionable about people who are *officially homeless*, something that degrades the experience of urban life and, indeed, the experience of riding public transit. It is for this reason (though not only for this reason) that homelessness ought to be an issue of communal concern.

Official estimates place the number of homeless people in Dallas County at 4,538, and of them, I must have encountered two or three hundred over the course of the past month alone, oftentimes on or around the various trains and stations of Dallas's light rail network. As a matter of fact, it is highly unusual that I board a train or wait on a platform without seeing two or three conspicuous Trevors. According to figures from the Metro Dallas Homeless Alliance, more than three quarters of this population comprise men, and more than two-thirds are between the ages of twenty-five and thirty-four. This seems about right to me.

Based on what I've observed, I doubt that the Trevors I've encountered are actually set on going anywhere. They are riding on a train, but they are not *taking public transit* in any meaningful sense. When they board and take a seat or curl up on the dirty floor next to the heater, they do so without regard for time or terminus.

They are commonly shrouded in a ball of tattered sleeping bag, blanket, and cloth that makes it impossible for them to see anything and impossible for anyone to see them. It's conceivable that in their darkness they are paying attention to the intercom's announcements of the upcoming stations, but the fact that I have never witnessed a single one of them disembark of their own volition makes that seem unlikely.

In this respect, DART is a mobile homeless shelter, a space where thousands of the poorest Dallasites congregate for refuge from the heat, the cold, or simply to sidestep accusations of loitering that would be made more forcefully if they were set up on a street corner or under an overpass. I suppose they figure that sleeping on the platform doesn't constitute loitering because "I'm waiting for the next train" is always at the ready, and camping out on a vehicle doesn't constitute loitering because they are technically in motion relative to the world outside.

The people under the blankets are a good bunch to ride with, all things considered. They're generally quiet, and they keep to themselves, but the fact that they present as nothing more than an amorphous blob of fabric makes for an eerie dynamic if there is nobody else in the car, something I have experienced on many occasions. Looking at them for more than a few minutes, you begin to wonder how long it would take for someone to notice if they died. "Are they even alive right now?" you wonder to yourself. "What if I'm actually just riding the train right now with three corpses?" A bump in the tracks will jostle them from time to time, causing a visible readjustment and allowing those grim thoughts to dissipate, but reliably, there is a minute or two where the idea creeps in: they might be dead. Frankly, replacing these people with corpses wouldn't change the experience of riding in any discernible way.

But some of the homeless people on DART are more lively. Once every two or three rides, you'll encounter someone who paces up and down the aisle, aimlessly gesticulating, cursing under their breath, and sporadically singling out other riders to converse with. Only on rare occasions is a verbal response provided by the poor soul who has been singled out by the aimless gesticulator. Avoiding eye contact is one of the surest ways to prevent them from choosing you, but even the most guarded introverts are sometimes faced with unwelcome interactions. It can be incredibly unnerving when someone confronts you on the train.

I was riding to work one weekday morning on the Green Line, with service terminating at North Carrollton/Frankford station. This, for any Metroplexers who may be interested, is the line on which most of my DART experiences are based, although my time riding the Red, Blue, and Orange leads me to believe that it's fairly representative of the network as a whole. Like most days, the car was roughly a quarter filled—mostly by the homeless or quasi-homeless, but also by a sizable medley of construction men and food service workers, groggy, solemn-looking people with sunken eyes, crooked spines, and shapeless bodies.

It was a normal morning on DART. Some people were sleeping, some were twiddling their thumbs, and those who had them were staring down at their phones. As per usual, an upsetting bouquet of malt liquor, cigarette smoke, and unshowered bodies filled the air. I was tuned out, reveling in the seclusion afforded by my headphones. For what must have been the fifth consecutive morning, Texas's sweetheart was making the commute a truly golden hour, and that helped me forget about the varied material unpleasantries of the train. Mezzo-soprano magic.

Sadly, my little island of musically induced tranquility was about to be flooded by a monsoon of indecent exposure that is undeniably criminal but perfectly unsurprising when riding DART. In the reflection of the window, I noticed something at the other end of the car around the raised articulation that is found at each point where the trains are coupled. Turning toward the thing directly, I observed that it was a man who was coming, rather hurriedly, down the aisle in my direction. I'd put him somewhere between thirty and forty, although the damages of homelessness make estimations notoriously difficult. He stopped once, maybe thirty feet from me, and shouted something unintelligible, which jolted awake the rider in the nearest seat. The man was fairly normal-looking from the waist up. At least, he was normal-looking for the sort of person who tends to ride DART—scraggly and unkempt, but clothed in a T-shirt. He was not wearing shoes or socks, but there were a pair of athletic shorts held up just slightly above his knees. Between his knees and his waist, there was nothing. This guy was just walking around the train with everything, save his torso and shins, on display.

He continued a few rows closer, still yelling things that everyone on the train could hear, but that I seriously doubt anyone could understand. Those in the rows ahead of me were wisely resisting the impulse to stare. Of course, this is an iron law of successful public transit ridership: you never look at the person who is causing a scene. It's tough. An uncomfortable Medusa-esque dynamic always seems to emerge when you know you're close to someone who is poised to fly off the handle. The natural human instinct is to study them, as a precaution, and also out of sheer curiosity. But you can't ever give in. You make eye contact and you're screwed.

I knew this rule as well as anyone, and like those in front me, I averted my gaze and did my best to pretend I didn't see him. But for whatever reason, he decided to approach me, continuing to blather as he did so. It was one of those indescribably tense moments where you can feel that someone is looking at you, even if you're not looking at them.

He got closer, row by row, until he was finally within an arm's length from me. Out of my peripheral vision, it was clear that this man's uncovered parts were now egregiously close to me and that he was not going to continue down the aisle until the two of us exchanged words.

"You gah fuh lie?" he shouted, proving that my noise-canceling headphones would be better described as noise-reducing. I didn't really know what he was asking, but I suspected it was a question based on the way he produced an outstretched hand, as if he were a train conductor asking for my ticket. I was on edge, but I figured that the Medusa rule shouldn't change just because Medusa's dick, balls, and naked ass are hanging out or because Medusa is very likely to be high on crystal meth. If anything, that only makes the imperative more important.

"You gah fuh lie!?" the man repeated, this time louder than before, shaking his hand closer to my face.

I tried not to cave.

"YOU GAH FUH'N LIE?"

He was now seriously overpowering my music. Also, I was beginning to wonder if pretending not to notice him would only aggravate the situation. This guy's hand was too close to me. What if he just snapped and punched me or something? He was definitely on some sort of stimulant.

"AYY, MANG, I AHHIN YOU GAH FUH'N LIE?" He lunged forward, puffing his chest out, and his penis swung toward me, making it clear that these inquiries were not rhetorical, nor would they be abandoned without a formal response. I had seen enough. I had to say something. Medusa had won.

I took off my headphones and turned away from the window, facing him directly for the first time.

"Excuse me?" I replied, as amicably and sincerely as I could manage.

"I AHHIN YOU IH YOU GAH A FUH'N LIE MANG," he put back to me, just as loudly as he had when I was listening to music. He appeared both indignant and surprised that I was having difficulty understanding him.

"A lie?"

"YEAH, MANG, FUH," he nodded as he brought his other arm toward his mouth pretending to take a drag of a cigarette.

Ahhh, a *lighter*. I should have realized. It's a pretty common request. Although in retrospect, the man did seem to be missing a number of teeth, so I suppose this phonemic handicap and my confusion were both understandable.

"Ohhh. No, sorry. I don't." I said, thinking that this would set him on route down the aisle to try his luck with the next guy he picked out. I was wrong.

"Da fuh, you mean? You don' smoe?" he queried, skeptically, shorts still around knees, genitals still completely exposed.

"No. I don't, sorry."

What a bizarre thing to be conversing with an unclad junkie on the train to work. How many people like me had already been subjected to this man earlier in the morning?

"Sheeeet, at's some fuh'd up sheet. You trippin? You lyin' to me?"

I stared at him, dead in the eye. "No. I don't smoke."

Then there was silence between us for a brief moment or two as he considered my response. A woman across the car had been observing the exchange. She offered me a subtle, sympathetic glance, as if to say, "I'm sorry he chose you. That's a bummer." I was also sorry, but I felt as though I had indulged him for long enough, so I placed the headphones back over my ears and turned my head to face the window.

Unfortunately, the faint reflection produced by the glass meant that I could still see the man standing in the aisle, staring down at me. To my great chagrin, he hadn't pulled up his shorts in the intervening seconds. What was he thinking in those moments? Did he actually think I was lying to him? What was the lighter for? I've seen people smoking weed and cigarettes on the train, but again, he struck me as being under the influence of something much more formidable.

His staring lasted for a period of around fifteen seconds that felt like fifteen minutes, at which point he released a parting grunt and then pivoted down the aisle, presumably to test the charity of the other riders, many of whom would undoubtedly have lighters to spare.

One might be tempted to assume that this sort of bizarre encounter is much more common in the evening than in the morning. My own experience, however, leads me to believe that the frequency of such engagements actually has little to do with the time of day. I have ridden the final train at midnight, the first train at 5 a.m., and spent miserable hours at platforms in the intervening window. The tumult aboard and around DART is, unfortunately, a 24/7 phenomenon.

And while this was one of the more unsettling confrontations I've had on the train, it is hardly a rarity. I'm positive that if I had polled the other riders on the car that morning, many would have been able to provide me with tales of wayward debauchery that made mine seem banal and relatively trivial. DART is the Wild West. On any given day, you are almost certain to see people on drugs, consuming drugs, buying drugs, or selling drugs, and engaging in all of the degeneracy attendant to such behavior.

And, of course, therein lies a central problem with the city's public transit: the average citizen views it as a grubby haunt for delinquency of every conceivable flavor. They're not wrong. This is not a delusional perspective. A single, twenty-four-year-old man can deal with it by plugging his nose and keeping to himself, but not everyone is quite so lucky. If you're a Dallasite with kids, you avoid public transit like the plague, for the same reason you would avoid a family trip to the neighborhood brothel, heroin den, or supervised consumption site. It's not good for children to grow up around people getting high and turning tricks.

From the conversations that I have had with parents in the Metroplex, whether they be Gen-Xers who live in the suburbs or older millennials who live in townhouses within the city limits, not riding DART on the grounds of safety and propriety is a foregone conclusion.

"DART's a little bit sketchy," one woman from Richardson warned me. "There's a station five minutes from my house, but I would never take it, even if I couldn't drive. I would rather take a cab. There are just some … errrr … I've been told that there are some sketchy folks on trains and buses. And you can see them doing all sorts of things when you drive past the bus stops and train stations. Bad things, dear. You know what I mean."

I did know what she meant and so does everyone else in this city.

Another man extended a similar admonition. "I've ridden it once. I remember taking it to go see a Mavericks game a few years back. Honestly, I think it would've been better to just Uber or drive and then cough up the $10 or $15 for parking. There were a bunch of drunken bums, some of them passed out on the floor and a lot of them will panhandle and harass you for change. I definitely wouldn't take it to a game with my kids."

Millions of Dallasites will not ride DART because they view it as a homeless shelter on wheels where drugs and sex are swapped with total abandon and where the basic behavioral precepts of civil society are categorically absent. They may have no firsthand experience with the system itself, but they aren't entirely wrong.

CHAPTER 3

No Ads

THE WAYS YOU CAN GAUGE the wealth of DART's ridership are far too numerous to be fully described in a single chapter or, for that matter, a single book. There are the ragged clothes, the bare feet, the abominable odors, the raveled beards, and the countless other hallmarks of chronic poverty. But the truth is, you could be the only person in the city to show up to ride transit one day, and the setting would still provide an obvious tell that the people who normally use the service are completely broke. If everyone who normally rode DART suddenly vanished from the face of the earth, the stops, platforms, and vehicle walls alone would be enough to tell you everything you could possibly hope to know about their financial condition.

Riding the Tube in London, the Metro in Paris, or the Subway in New York City, you are immersed in a thoroughly consumeristic experience from the moment you descend down a station's escalators. You are shown big, bright advertisements selling everything from iPhones to ice cream, everything from concerts to kombucha. That new Netflix original your friends have been raving about?

You see the release date every morning on your commute to the office. The new abstract art exhibit you promised to go see with your significant other? Placards line the station walls with times and ticket prices. Glossy posters, vibrant murals, and phosphorescent, wall-sized screens all compete for your attention and for the attention of the hundreds of thousands of eyes that pass them by every single day. Whatever the format, marketing departments of major corporations, NGOs, and government bureaus will gladly fork out large sums of cash to feature their campaigns on mass transit networks like the aforementioned. This is, quite clearly, because they have reason to believe that some sizable contingent of these riderships are both willing and able to purchase their products. There is a justifiable expectation held by the marketer that the people taking these trains are going to or returning from a job. And based on the number of ads for brands like Breitling and Balenciaga, there is reason to believe that many of these people are going to or returning from jobs that pay exceedingly well.

Indeed, many of the people who ride transit in these places are quite well-off. In London, it is highly likely that a neurosurgeon living in a Pimlico townhouse and working at a Holborn hospital will take the Tube. A Parisian magnate working out of a skyscraper in La Défense would surprise no one by riding the Metro to and from his apartment in the 3rd arrondissement. And even in New York, it is not uncommon to see people of considerable means riding the Subway, not merely as a novelty, but as a matter of pragmatism.

While our world's advertising landscape is increasingly digital, it does still make sense to run physical ads on the Tube, the Metro, and the Subway, particularly in the space between pedestrian entrances and the gap where people are least likely to be staring at their phones.

In Dallas the walls are bare. They're bare on the platforms, and they're bare on the interior of the train cars and buses.

On the one hand, there's something almost cathartic about the brief intermission from the constant stream of corporate messaging that exists everywhere else in the world. On the other hand, it's always discouraging to notice the barren walls and remember that you and all the people you're riding with are not worth selling to. In their eyes, your tastes and proclivities are unimportant. You're not giving them money, so you don't matter. And when the bareness is appreciated in this way, it's much less a respite from passive consumerism and much more a reminder of your bleak socioeconomic irrelevance.

Though technically, the walls are not quite bare. It's worse than that. It's not that there is *nothing* on the walls. There are a few posters and notices, but they are almost always issued by DART itself rather than any external firm. Here are just a few examples of what you are likely to read while riding this city's public transit.

In big, bold print, on the panels above the seats:

> *Code of Conduct. DART has adopted a CODE OF CONDUCT to enhance the safety and comfort of all persons riding DART vehicles, using its facilities or visiting its properties. Section 2.02, part A, number 4 prohibits a person from engaging in disruptive, disturbing behavior including: loud conversation, profanity or rude insults, or operating any electronic device used for sound without an earphone(s). The consequences of violating this regulation may include being warned and/or ordered to leave DART property. Refusal to do so may result in the involvement of DART Police or other appropriate law enforcement agencies.*

The operative word in this warning is the "may" in that last sentence. Violation *may* result in law enforcement in the same way that cavalier pedestrians *may* be issued jaywalking citations. It's a reality that's true only in the most technical sense. Regular riders know that these behaviors are a dependable feature of any commute, and I, personally, have never seen authorities intervene to enforce this supposed COC. In my experience, no fist fight or boombox has been so large or loud as to trigger a response from DART Police. More on this in Chapter 5.

On a poster hung above the reserved handicapped and elderly seating:

> *Human trafficking in America is modern day slavery. Forced labor, sex trafficking, domestic servitude: it's happening in our community. Get informed. To report suspected trafficking, call 1-866-347-2423. For victim support, call 1-888-373-7888.*

On another poster adjacent the train doors:

> *Respete el viajie. Se prohíben pedir limosna y la venta ambulante. Fometar estas actividades lo puede poner en riesgo.* [This loosely translates to "Respect the trip. Begging and panhandling are prohibited. Encouraging these activities can put you at risk."]

It's common to see the ads in both languages—about as common as it is to see people begging and panhandling. What's there to lose? These people clearly aren't the sort to be dissuaded by the mealy mouthed copy of a middling comms intern.

On the metallic door of the enclosed driver's compartment:

> *Assaulting a DART employee is a felony. Violators will be prosecuted to the full extent of the law.*

As the great American adman Leo Burnett once remarked, "Good advertising doesn't just circulate information. It penetrates the public mind with desires and belief." Throughout the 1950s and 1960s, Burnett's dogged commitment to that axiom produced such unfading commercial icons as Tony the Tiger, Toucan Sam, the Pillsbury Doughboy, and, perhaps most illustriously, the Marlboro Man. This was a man who truly understood and appreciated the import of the subliminal in shaping popular sentiment.

The DART notices described above, according to Burnett's conception, are "good advertising" in that they effectively circulate information to the ridership. Even if riders contravene the directives *en masse*, as is so consistently the case, the principal purpose of the notices is achieved. The explicit information is made clear to anyone who can read, as well as to anyone who can hear the intercom announcements that reiterate warnings every few minutes. But moreover, and much more importantly, the notices are also "good advertising" in that they *do* penetrate the public mind with desires and beliefs: chiefly, the desire to avoid riding DART and the belief that DART is unmanageably chaotic. This desire is understandable because the belief is based very firmly in reality. What is being advertised by DART, so effectively yet so unintentionally, is the fact that social disorder is an inescapable feature of their service. When first-time riders are bombarded with knowledge of the criminal penalties for assaulting a driver, they rightly wonder why such a warning would be necessary, and the short mental exercise that follows is quite often enough to prevent them from becoming second-time riders.

There is, after all, a long list of protected demographics for whom it is a felony to assault. One of these demographics is the elderly.

What would be your reaction if you were touring assisted living facilities with a grandparent and you noticed that all of the bedroom doors were outfitted with big signs that read, "REMINDER: ASSAULTING A SENIOR CITIZEN IS A FELONY. NURSES AND AIDS MAY BE PROSECUTED"?

There's nothing wrong with the actual statement, per se, but the implication is unsettling; the signs wouldn't be there if issues hadn't arisen in the past, nor would they be there if management didn't anticipate issues arising in the future. People are suspicious of unsolicited information forcefully provided, and they tend to be quite good at reading between the lines.

When ads from organizations other than DART itself are visible on trains and buses, they usually publicize services like STD testing clinics. I've always found these sorts of ads strange, as they simply provide a phone number, website, or physical address below an enquiring "Chlamidya? Gonorrhea? Syphilis? We can help!" Or, bluntly and commandingly, "Get checked for STDs!" There are, thank God, no nightmarishly graphic depictions of blisters or pus, just a few lines of contact information.

I do wonder if this sort of thing leads to more people seeking medical help. If it does, I have severely underestimated the human capacity for nonchalance. I mean, imagine walking around knowing there's a high likelihood that you've contracted some sort of venereal disease. You know you've been, for lack of a better term, unsafe. Days turn into weeks, which turn into months, until one day, as you are riding DART from God knows where to God knows where else, you notice the ad. A light flickers on in the back of your mind. "Oh yeah," you think to yourself, "I've been in excruciating pain every time I've taken a piss for the past few weeks. I guess I should probably get that checked out."

Granted, there are a number of other precautionary reasons why someone might feel compelled to get tested for STDs, but it seems incredibly difficult to believe that the prospect would only occur after a chance encounter on public transit. I'm not convinced these ads do much for public health. They seem ineffectual and misapplied.

Conversely, there's an ad that I came across not too long ago at Royal Lane Station that struck me as brilliant in its placement. It was one of the only other non-DART campaigns I've seen so far.

In big gold letters on a striking magenta billboard, immediately across from where the train doors open:

Donating Plasma + BioLife DFW = Earn up to $700 in your first month

Something about this one felt slimy and uncomfortable from the moment I laid eyes on it. There was something about it that troubled me and gave me pause in a way that none of the other ads did. For a few days, I wasn't quite sure why. I passed the billboard every morning, each time wondering why it seemed so wrong. After all, plasma is an exceptionally valuable resource on which thousands depend for life-saving treatments. If a willing adult freely elects to exchange their own body fluids for money, surely they should be permitted to do so. In some sense, it's not all that different from a day laborer swapping his sweat for a small sum of cash, and I wouldn't take the same exception to an ad from a landscaper. Ostensibly, each case involves two parties executing a legitimate, contractually fortified transaction.

And yet this veneer of consent erodes with the most cursory review of a typical donor's conditions and motivations. Consider, for instance, the following findings from a Cleveland-based study conducted by the Center for Health Care Research and Policy (CHCRP) on the demographic characteristics of regular plasma donors: 77 percent of donors spend their payment on food; 57 percent of donors receive over a third of their regular income from donating plasma; and 57 percent of donors are unemployed.[2]

The study also analyzed the relationship between the states' minimum wage and plasma donors per capita. As one might expect, none of the eight states with the most plasma donors per capita (Texas among them) had a minimum wage above the federal floor of $7.25, and eleven out of the twelve states with the least plasma donors per capita did. This seems fairly perverse. Worse still, as Texas is both the state with the most people who fall within the healthcare coverage gap and the state with the most plasma donors, many of the people who supply plasma to companies would not be able to afford the life-saving treatments made possible by their own contributions.

First of all, this wolfish somatic exploitation of the working and unworking poor is gross and should make everyone feel sick, purely on moral and egalitarian grounds. But it also threatens the integrity of the plasma supply and the health of all those who rely upon it. The same CHCRP study revealed that 70 percent of donors experienced a medical side effect such as weakness, bruising, dehydration, or fainting; that 30 percent use prescription/OTC medicines for asthma, pain relief, HTN, diabetes, and depression; and that 13 percent have misled plasma center workers about their medical history in order to donate. People who live below the poverty line will lie on a form to get some cash. Who could've guessed?

Admittedly, the solution probably isn't as simple as removing the financial incentives. Countries like Australia and the UK, for example, do not allow paid donations and in turn rely heavily on US imports, a dynamic that has popularized America's status as the OPEC of plasma products. America's primacy as the global supplier of plasma has become so entrenched and so widely recognized that there's now a substantial influx of Mexicans crossing the border on temporary visas for the sole purpose of paid donation. These are the sorts of cruelties one spends their time mulling over on the train.

I don't think there's an especially attractive or just solution here. Insofar as blood plasma is subject to the same blunt economic pressures as any other commodity, and insofar as America allows companies to solicit donations in exchange for cash, it's only reasonable to assume that the poorest among us will continue to rely on draining themselves to meet their basic needs. And I suppose that's what I found so unpleasant about the ad: how brazenly it exposed and capitalized on the destitution of the people who are forced to ride the train. It's a soul-sucking thing to look at every morning. Plasma has to come from somewhere. I get it. I guess I just can't get over how nauseating it is, how unapologetically predatory and inhumane it all feels.

I wonder how the conversations played out at the BioLife corporate office when decisions were being made about how best to attract new donors. Surely everything was coated with a fluffy layer of corporate valleyspeak and decided upon by a gaggle of hyper-sanitized suburbanites who have never ridden transit in their own city and who wouldn't dream of doing so in Dallas:

> So, Morgan, I was thinking about settings for the new ad. What if we, like, invested more in outreach toward community partners who, like, rely on alternative forms of transit. Because, if they don't have access to a car or whatever, then they're probably totally low SES and that's, like, low-key our market segment.
>
> That's a really good idea, Jenna. Those folx would definitely be about it. No frequency cap, high stickiness. Our CPM would pop off, but, like, in real life. Love that for them. Love that for us.
>
> Yassss, queen. They could definitely use help, like, getting their bag and I'm 100 percent here for it.

It must have gone something like that. Shameless succubi. Oh, to work in advertising.

I'm no Burnett, but it seems rather plain to me that good advertising is also about dangling something in front of an audience that they will find tempting. If you pay attention to the objects that litter the property of DART, it's quite easy to determine which goods occupy the minds of the ridership.

A typical station, be it at grade or elevated, is speckled with an assortment of refuse and paraphernalia that grows acutely familiar after mere days of riding. The most common items include twenty-five-fluid-ounce cans of either Bud Ice, King Cobra, Bush Signature, Hurricane, or Colt 45, sometimes shrouded in brown paper bags, but just as often exposed; Swisher Sweets wrappers; cigarette butts; JUULpod cartridges; used condoms; soda bottles filled with urine; half-eaten containers of fast food; empty Nicorette packets; frayed sleeping bags; scratched lottery tickets; and spent hypodermic needles. As an unsavory aside, there is also an appalling volume of excrement spattered upon random objects like T-shirts and raggedy tote bags.

Needless to say, these places are viscerally and aesthetically revolting. The odors are especially bad in the summer, and the general snowlessness of Texan winters means the aforementioned miscellany of trash is visible twelve months a year. The property of DART is basically all just one big *unsupervised* injection site, and if ad campaigns were truly aligned with the spending habits of the ridership, that's what would be pushed on the billboards. "Your dealer charging you too much? We've got you covered! Text xxx-xxx-xxxx for the lowest prices in DFW!"

Seeing it up close is pretty brutal. One time on the Green Line, I shared a car with the most tormented girl I have ever seen. She boarded at Akard Station, and the way she did so reminded me of someone nervously venturing onto a frozen lake in late spring. Her first step off of the platform was very slow, like she was applying pressure to make sure she wouldn't plunge through the floor; then a little quicker with the next; the third step quicker still, until she gradually moved at a normal pace to a seat roughly fifteen feet from myself. And yet, it wasn't her cagey stride that caught my attention; it was the abrupt, twitching movement of her arms and torso, as if every step required a spasmodic jerk to stabilize her upper half.

She was a rather thin woman—something that was easily ascertained despite the billowing cotton poncho in which she hid herself. I could tell because the pant legs of her dark skinny jeans looked like they were wrapped around yardsticks. Even among people who are particularly top-heavy, there's a certain circumference of the thigh that indicates encompassing waifishness. Indeed, she was a truly skinny woman, not just skinny by Texas standards.

But I could also tell that she was skinny from her face alone. It was still dark outside, but the strained yellow lights seeping down from the car's ceiling were enough to outline her bony features. Her cheeks were distinctly fleshless and concave, which gave the impression that she was perpetually sucking through some imaginary, microscopic straw. Her jawline was boyishly angular, simultaneously sharp and fragile. Her lips were large, almost swollen, and they quivered in sync with the aforementioned convulsions. I was able to see this because, like many of the other passengers, she was not wearing a mask—perhaps deliberately, but more likely due to an overwhelming preoccupation with whatever had produced her current condition. The pandemic that had turned the world upside down for so many billions was trivial to her. She had bigger problems.

Her jet-black hair was ratty and unkempt. It seemed likely that she was sleeping on the streets and occasionally in the backseats and bedrooms of strange, lecherous men. She reeked of exhaustion—probably of menthol cigarettes, as well, although the wretched odor of the train made confirming such a thing nearly impossible.

And still, in her own way, she was beautiful, with intensely compelling eyes. The only thing about her that looked stable or robust were her eyes. They were a bold, auburn color—bright, especially in contrast to the deep purple bags atop which they sat. At the risk of sounding melodramatic, they were the sort of inexpressibly sincere eyes that seemed to tell a much more forceful and descriptive biography than words ever could. They were those iconic Afghan Girl eyes that make for convincing humanitarian ads and public murals that the public actually enjoys. They were alive and gripping, but tremendously sad.

Even after sitting down, the abrupt movements of her upper body continued. For five minutes or so, I watched her writhing back and forth like she was trapped in a fit of night terrors that wouldn't end by waking up. West End Station passed, then Victory. It was still rather early, though the car was much fuller than usual. There must have been fifteen of us on board, including a large man of approximately thirty sitting next to me. He looked drowsy and worn out, but he, too, was watching the sudden movements of the woman.

Then the shaking eased, ever so slightly, and the woman plunged her sleeveless arm deep into the poncho. When she took it out, we could see that she was clutching an orange-capped needle filled with a murky brown fluid. I cocked an eyebrow and tilted my head toward the man next to me. I didn't say anything, but my expression must have been as clear as if I had actually asked aloud, "Are we about to watch this girl mainline smack on the morning commute?" The man returned my look with a slight nod and then leaned back in his seat, facially unbothered.

As it happens, that was exactly what we were about to watch. She gave her arm a cursory inspection, ensuring that it was still attached to her body, and then punctured her skin with the needle's tip. Steadily, her thumb pushed down on the syringe until the entire dose had been consumed. And the shaking stopped, and the woman let out a long, relieved sigh. It was as if she were just given an epipen after an intense anaphylactic episode or a breath of air after thrashing underwater.

I looked again at the man across from me to see his reaction, but he had since lost interest and was now peering out the window. Dozens of times he must have seen things this grotesque. He struck me as the sort of man who had been riding the train for many years, long enough that the sight of someone slamming heroin at 6 a.m. on a weekday was no longer enough to pique his interest.

While the initial moments of the high were inevitably a release from what she was enduring beforehand, it wasn't long before the catharsis began to fade. The shallow look of relief that clung to her bony face as the liquefied tar circulated her body quickly reverted to one of volatility and despair; she now looked just as she had when first boarding the train. Whatever artificial placidity she had shot proved good for only a few fleeting moments of respite. Though perhaps the perception of respite was merely artificial as well. Perhaps her phenomenological experience had not changed at all throughout my observation, only her outward display. Much like the practicality of Purell-based cocktails, I ruminated over this thought for a second or two before realizing how utterly and completely stupid it was to waste energy on something so inconsequential. It didn't really matter. I was on a train that was far too cold and smelled far too much like urine for any clear thinking to get done.

The misery continued. It was hardly two minutes after the injection before she began to sob uncontrollably. Tears trickled down her cadaverous face and into the palms of her scraggy hands, which sat facing upward on her lap. Yet even as her crying intensified, the violent arm movements had not returned. It almost seemed like they were glued to her thighs. I vaguely remembered reading something about this in college: one of the immediate effects of heroin is a sensation of heaviness in the limbs. Back then, I imagined that it must have felt like waking up to find all of your blood replaced with cement in your sleep, sort of like how you feel the morning after a very long run or a ferocious night of drinking. Neither of those situations seemed quite analogous to what this woman was going through, though. I simply could not imagine what she felt. I could not imagine what it would be like to be weighed down by arms as light as hers—what it would be like to hold an anvil that didn't exist.

Doing heroin must feel amazing. I mean, these people are really destroying themselves.

If you've spent considerable time in a big city, you've seen people do heroin. It's an unremarkable spectacle, mostly, after you've seen it enough. You have places to go and things to do. Occasionally you'll notice the individuals, their lamentable features and peculiarities, but overwhelmingly, they become the sort who blend in as nondescript characteristics of the urban gestalt. There's nothing perceptibly idiosyncratic about them to the average passerby. And normally, I am an average passerby.

But there was something distinctly humanizing about this woman. Something uniquely deserving of attention and demanding of empathy. As she sat there with her ethereally leaden arms hanging out the holes of her poncho, magnificent eyes now stormy with little saline globules, I thought about my sister.

This might sound trite and uninteresting. But I don't simply mean that I imagined my sister being addicted to heroin and then tried to conjure up some sort of lame introspection. Rather, I imagined her becoming addicted to heroin. I imagined the process.

See, it's quite meaningless for most moneyed people to imagine a loved one being a heroin addict because the notion seems so extravagant and unlikely. It seems like nothing more than a trivial thought experiment because it contrasts so sharply with real life as experienced by you, the sort of endowed, fortunate soul who is likely to be reading creative non-fiction for leisure.

Yet it becomes less far-fetched and more emotionally salient when you actually pause and envision the specifics of what such a tragic descent might involve. I was still on a train that was far too cold and smelled far too much like urine, but this thought was something that held my attention. As we rode from station to station, I sat there and actually imagined the deterioration of my sister's life to the depths of the woman who sat before me, tortured by circumstance and rag-dolled by happenings beyond her control. I imagined the chance missteps and cruel twists of fate that would need to occur, realized that they could, realized how often they in fact do, and it made me nauseous. If you're someone with a colorful imagination and a sister or daughter, you can try this out and see what I mean.

The woman continued to cry. Whose sister was she? Whose daughter? Was she a mother, too? Analogous questions could be asked of the mimosa man who pissed himself at the bus stop. What a nightmarish thought! What a nightmarish scene! What a nightmarish morning! And what a nightmarish reality that on the buses and trains of Dallas and on those throughout this spectacularly twisted nation, the world's "shining city on a hill," there are countless people like him, people like her, and problems like these.

CHAPTER 4

Lots of Track

THE PUBLIC AVERSION TO DART would not be all that remarkable if the system were as small as its ridership would suggest. If DART were comprised of a mile-long tram line supplemented by a dozen bus routes, it wouldn't really matter what people thought of it or at what capacity it was utilized. But DART is huge. Despite the fact that Dallasites tend to avoid riding public transit, their city's infrastructure is not at all insignificant.

In order to appreciate the prevalence of the experiences conveyed in this book, it's useful to have a sense of the network's vastness.

DART's rail network is an incredibly large system serving much of the sprawling Dallas–Fort Worth Metroplex. The rail network is made up of ninety-three miles of light rail and a single modern street car line, covering a geographic area of over 700 square miles and serving thirteen cities in the North Texas region. DART's rail network consists of four primary light rail lines: the Red Line, Blue Line, Green Line, and Orange Line, and a single street car line, the D-Link.

The Red Line, which began service in 1996, runs from Westmoreland Station in West Dallas to Parker Road Station in

Plano, covering a distance of twenty-eight miles. The Blue Line, which began service in 1990, runs from Ledbetter Station in South Dallas to Rowlett Station in Rowlett, covering a distance of thirty-one miles. The Green Line, which began service in 2009, runs from Buckner Station in southeast Dallas to Carrollton Station in Carrollton, covering a distance of twenty miles. The Orange Line, which began service in 2012, runs from DFW Airport Station in Irving to Parker Road Station in Plano, covering a distance of fourteen miles. The D-Link street-car line, which began service in 2015, runs from Union Station to Bishop Arts District, covering a distance of 1.6 miles.

Connected by its sixty-five stations, DART is the longest light rail network in the country.

There's a lot of track, and the city is getting very little out of it.

In 2021, DART's light rail ridership was 14.5 million. Los Angeles, by comparison, saw a 2021 ridership of 47,866,883[3] on its Metro Rail system, which is only eight miles longer than DART's network and actually shorter if its twenty-two miles of heavy rail subway are excluded.

Indeed, Angelinos makes much better use of their trains than do Dallasites, and LA is hardly a city known for its adoption of public transit.

The up-front development costs incurred over the past three decades to build this network have been staggering. According to a report by the Federal Transit Administration, the total cost for the initial construction of the twenty-mile starter system, which opened in 1996, was approximately $3.5 billion. This included the cost of building the Red Line from Westmoreland to Pearl/Arts District, the Blue Line from Illinois Station to Garland, and the Green Line from Victory Station to Pleasant Grove.

Subsequent extensions to the light rail lines, such as the Orange Line, which extends from Downtown Dallas to DFW International

Airport, and the Cotton Belt Line, which connects with DFW Airport, have added additional costs to the system. The total cost for the Orange Line, for example, was approximately $1.3 billion.

The DART bus network is similarly massive, consisting of 692 buses servicing 6,878 stops along approximately ninety routes, covering a vast geographic area of over 700 square miles and serving thirteen cities in the North Texas region. The routes vary in length, with some covering short distances within city limits, while others travel long distances, connecting suburban communities to downtown Dallas and other city centers. DART's 2021 estimated bus ridership was 20.1 million, much less, again, than comparably populous cities with shorter network lengths.[4]

Keeping such an extensive network running is, unsurprisingly, very costly. According to DART's report for the fiscal year 2021, the organization's total annual expenses, which included vehicle operating costs, salaries for its 3,762 employees, infrastructure maintenance, and administration, were $954 million.[5]

All of this is to say that despite being used by a trivially small proportion of Dallasites, and despite providing little economic return for the city, DART is massive, in terms of both its physical size and financial cost.

DART is a forgotten feature of the urban landscape to most people, but the buses and trains are there by the hundreds.

The incidents I'm describing and their glaring social corollaries are, to be sure, playing out on a far larger scale than most people realize.

CHAPTER 5

Blood from Stones

FEBRUARY 2021 SAW TEXAS HIT by a winter storm that caused pipes and gas lines to burst, freeways to become unnavigable, and large swaths of the state's power grid to be knocked offline for hours or even days at a time, leaving millions of people to shelter in place in cold, dark homes.

The storm received widespread media coverage, and many American politicos spoke out about top Republicans being caught offside for their uncannily hypocritical positions and behaviors. Texas Attorney General Ken Paxton had just recently denounced Californian Democrats for politicizing and mismanaging their state's grid amidst a crippling heatwave; a former state governor claimed on FOX News that Texans would be willing to endure longer blackouts in order to "keep the federal government out of their business"; and, most notoriously, junior US Senator Ted Cruz slipped away from the chaos of his home state to the Ritz-Carlton Cancun for a week of rest and rejuvenation. Now, as a fellow Albertan masquerading as a Texan (Cruz is from Calgary) who would have rather spent that week cupping cocktails and soaking up rays on the Yucatán Peninsula,

I certainly understand the impulse. Like millions of people across the state, I spent hours and even days at a time without basic utilities like heat, electricity, water, and, most critically, Wi-Fi. Granted, I'm not a sitting member of the US Senate, so I suppose my pining for warmer climes in the midst of a generational crisis isn't quite the indictment.

Uri and the ensuing blackouts left many people criticizing the absurdity of Texas's uniquely fragile system. Questions were raised about whether energy providers should be allowed to peg rates to wholesale market prices, and how such critical infrastructure could be so vulnerable to the caprices of nature, and why regulatory bodies like the Texas Public Utilities Commission were allowed to dissolve their oversight and enforcement arm in 2020. In short, people wanted to know why the lights went out and whose bottom line was achieved at the expense of the average Joe. It was a brutal week, and it fostered widespread public support for inquiry and reform.

But the event also served as a reminder of something far more mundane and apolitical: Texas can get cold. Nowhere in the state ever gets truly, intensely cold by global standards, but it does get cold enough to make life outdoors profoundly unpleasant. The lowest point that the mercury ever dipped was –17°C, just 6°C above the city's lowest recorded temperature, a sort of cold that is unremarkable in northern states but that turns a city like Dallas on its head. Normal winter temperatures range from nighttime lows of around 2°C to daytime highs of around 15°C. It's not the kind of raw, biting cold that should have one concerned about frostbite or anything like that, but it is sufficiently cold that the homeless people are compelled indoors. By the looks of things on DART, few better options exist than the train.

As I've said previously, you're likely to see dozens of homeless people using the train as a temporary shelter whenever taking the train, and the numbers are especially high in the cooler months between December and March. The cars aren't particularly well insulated, and the constant opening and closing of the doors introduces the outside air at every stop. Still, the small, metallic radiators just above the floor give off enough heat to keep the interior at a temperature perceptibly higher than outside. Were I to ever find myself as a homeless man in this city, unable to access charitable shelters for whatever reason, squatting on the train would probably occupy much of my time, by necessity. Perhaps there would be nowhere else to go.

DART has some advantages over, say, homeless shelters. There are no *real* rules on the train like there are in shelters. Homelessness is largely a consequence of not being able to abide by society's rules, and shelters, for all the good that they do, often enforce a regiment of such rules that disqualify many of the people I encountered on DART.

Dallas Life, on Cadiz and Griffin, is an illustrative example. They're doing wonderful work, by all accounts, yet the intake restrictions they impose for the sake of operational sustainability undoubtedly preclude thousands of the roughest, most despondent Dallasites from accessing services. Among other guidelines, residents must

- present ID and a Social Security card;
- not be on parole;
- not have a prior conviction resulting from a sexual or violent crime;
- not fraternize with other residents;
- not keep pets;
- subject themselves to random drug testing.

Anyone who believes these preconditions to be peripheral or inconsequential lacks the most basic familiarity with those who wander the streets of major American metropolises like Dallas. I would bet everything I own that a majority of the loiterers on DART fail to satisfy at least two of these criteria. They are broken, tragic people who lead broken, tragic lives. And unfortunately, to find shelter at a place like Dallas Life, you really can't be all that broken or all that tragic. You're required to abide by a defined set of rules, and your personal history must be relatively unblemished. To get onto DART, all you need is a $2.50 ticket, and, honestly, you don't even need that.

"There are no free rides," warn the bright yellow signs within every car. "If you ride without paying, you could be charged with a Class C misdemeanor and fined," a reporting hotline conveniently provided below. I'm really not much of a gambler, but I would also bet everything I own that this hotline is seldom called.

Every few rides, a fare enforcement officer boards the train and performs a sweep of the cabin. Occasionally, a newbie will perk up when this happens, plunging a hand into their pocket as if proof of payment really were about to be validated. The overwhelming response from passengers, however, is a flagrant apathy best demonstrated by those who are entirely cloaked in their mound of tarnished blankets. To them, the enforcement officer is much like the cool draft that floats in through the open doors, hardly noticeable after hours spent in the same spot on the same car.

"Tickets, tickets, tickets," he will mutter as he paces the aisle, glancing side to side and offering an affirmative nod to the sleeping, lifeless lumps of body.

A select few oblige by producing a ticket that they paid for, one that is actually valid. More often than not though, riders either flash a crinkled, recycled ticket in the inspector's general direction, one that expired months ago, or they pretend that he doesn't exist, the latter resulting in escalation from the fare inspector only on the rarest occasions. Most fare inspectors don't care if people paid for a ticket, nor should they. Their jobs would be more miserable if they were actually expected to expel from the train all those who did not pay and more miserable still if they were actually expected to serve evaders with citations and fines.

Something like 80 percent of the ridership is without a valid ticket on any given train. Four out of five. The number has to be something like that. In the exceedingly rare instance where an enforcement officer objects to the evasion of a rider, this approximate exchange ensues:

"Where's your ticket? You need a ticket, sir."

"Ticket?"

"Yes, sir, a ticket."

"Fuck is you talkin' 'bout? Fuck outta' here. C'mon, man."

"Can't be ridin' on no train without no ticket, sir."

"Nah, man, c'mon, don't do me like that. Fuck that, man, you trippin'."

"That's the rules, sir. Get off at the next stop."

"You serious, man? You fuckin' serious?"

"Get off at the next stop," the officer repeats, assuring the rider of his seriousness.

Judging this to be far preferable to the alternative of actually receiving a citation for fare evasion, the individual will indeed get off at the next stop. If they actually were riding the train to get somewhere specific, they will just wait at the platform for the next train heading in that direction. If they were riding to nowhere, as so many are, they will either establish themselves horizontally on a platform bench or board the next train in the opposite direction, riding that line until its terminus or until they are kicked off by another enforcement officer.

There is an absurd futility to the fare enforcement process. It's a big charade. Watching the officers patrol the cars is like watching a man condemned to play a never-ending game of Whac-A-Mole with a nonexistent hammer. How anyone familiar with DART could fail to see this is beyond me.

Anything goes on this city's transit, in large part because the DART Police is a thoroughly toothless, profligate institution that consistently fails to ensure fare payment, constrain rider conduct, and enforce basic criminal laws. Those who board trains and buses in this city are greeted, quite reliably, by people selling drugs, playing loud music, fighting, exposing themselves, and finding countless other ways to establish an atmosphere of peril and pandemonium.

The disorder really isn't all the fault of DART. What are officers to do? A lot of these offenders (most, I suspect) don't even have valid IDs, which turns out to serve as a colossal impediment in the administration of justice. Writing a ticket to John Doe of 123 Main Street is easily one. If Mr. Doe is doing something criminal and if he can easily be identified by authorities, then leveraging the threat of future sanction against him is straightforward, imminently accessible, and therefore highly attractive to the average officer. But if this same criminal is without ID and if he makes himself known to officers simply as Johnny the pantsless junkie of no fixed address swearing at people on the Green Line, recourse becomes a more complicated, unappealing process. The latter man cannot be ticketed because law enforcement, and the state more generally, has little to no idea of who he really is. Without the ability to effectively ticket, therefore, mass arresting campaigns present as the only alternative to addressing petty crime, and there is neither the political will nor bureaucratic ability necessary to accomplish this in a city like Dallas, not by a long shot.

Besides the logistical complications attendant to anonymity, there's the bleak reality that many of the people who might otherwise be charged with criminal offenses have nothing to lose. They have no jobs to be fired from; no bank accounts to be drained; no wives, girlfriends, or families to be jilted by; no social network from which to be ostracized. They have nothing and will, in all likelihood, continue to have nothing for the rest of their lives.

So, it is sensible to ask questions about the relative quality of life out on the streets: Are these people leading richer, more satisfying lives than they would in the custody of the state? Is it meaningfully worse to be a prisoner than a drug-addled vagrant in a city as inhospitable as Dallas? Prisons are despairing places, to be sure, but they are also poised to deliver the material sufficiencies that are so painfully absent out there in the *free* world. For all that can be said of this nation's prisons, convicts eat better food, sleep on nicer beds, and are doctored to with far greater regard than the people you are likely to find quarreling with an officer of DART Police.

Given the choice between tramping around West End Station for a month and spending a month in prison, I'm fairly certain I would elect the latter. It would be a close call, in any case, and the threat of one over the other would influence my decision about as much as telling me that action X causes me to be gored by a unicorn, whereas action Y will cause the abominable snowman to rip my limbs out.

In a world of carrots and sticks, clear punishments and incentives are required to regulate behavior. Presently, no carrots are being dangled, and excessive hardship has rendered flogging completely ineffectual. Stated otherwise, reaction to the stick requires sensitivity, and the targets are largely desensitized. The citations for fare evasion range from $50 to $500, cosmically more money than any random DART rider is likely to have in liquid, disposable wealth, and the prospect of life behind bars isn't all that scary when you live as these people do. As a consequence, prosecuting the transgressions that make DART so unpleasant is like getting blood from stones.

This dynamic manifests everywhere in America—the bottom quintile running amok of collective norms. Antisocial behavior is a complex thing, but few variables provide the same degree of explanatory value as despair and indifference. It's a terrible combination, and it is very much the case, as the beleaguered observer of despair and indifference James Baldwin once remarked, that "the most dangerous creation of any society is the man who has nothing to lose." If the infrastructure in cities like Dallas continues to be filled with people who are not deterred by the threat of financial penalty on account of having no financial capital to forfeit and nowhere to go but up, then America will continue to be plagued by disorder, dysfunction, and criminality. Serious countries don't have an underclass that is, by way of their chronic impoverishment, unreceptive to fines and civil directives.

Riding DART makes it hard to believe this is a serious country.

CHAPTER 6

Please Don't Shoot Me

"DIS MUH'FUCKA GON' GET IT. On god, dis muh'fucka really gon' get it!"

I hoped that it wouldn't be me—hoped that I was not the muh'fucka he was talking about.

"On god, dis muh'fucka really gon' get it! I swear to fuckin' god he gon' get it."

The man was getting louder and palpably more upset. Again, I really hoped that I would not be the muh'fucka who was going to get it, but the sheer fact of my proximity kept me from completely eliminating that as a possibility. I was only a foot or two away, after all, and everyone else was at the front of the bus.

The man discharging the unaddressed threats was sitting in the row of seats behind me, dark, rimless sunglasses covering his eyes but clearly looking down toward his lap. He was wearing tattered jeans, oversized high-tops, and a black T-shirt with a vaguely familiar athletic logo that had faded just slightly past the point of recognizability. It was the sort of outfit that pretty zoomer girls will assemble with a mood board, hundreds of dollars, and haughty contempt for their zestless suburban parents. But this man was clearly wearing it out of earnest necessity. I was watching him in the reflection of my phone and had been doing so since he boarded the 486, three stops earlier. After a brief argument with the driver about something I could not hear, most likely unpaid fare, he had traipsed down the aisle and taken up a seat in the back row, at which point his forbidding monologue had started.

He was planning to shoot someone, I think, or at least he was planning to threaten to shoot someone. I realized that this was why he was looking down at his lap. In one hand were half a dozen sheeny gold-colored bullets, and in the other was a revolver that was being casually twirled around his index finger like a set of car keys. After every three or four twirls, he would open the cylinder and slide the bullets out of the chamber, and then back in again, and then out, and then back in again. At first, I wondered why he had a revolver instead of a regular semi-automatic pistol (like I suspected was the case of most urban American handgun owners), but this twirling behavior was so broodingly fixated that I almost believe he chose a multi-chambered gun for that reason alone. What he was doing would not have been possible with a Glock. More probably, the revolver was like the outfit: all he had access to. The man smelled of weed and liquor. He seemed intoxicated, so I suspect that he was less dexterous than he might have otherwise been. And while he still seemed able to manipulate the small bullets with relative ease, the twirling unsettled me. I imagined an unfortunate fumble depressing the trigger and boring a hole straight through my head. Surely, many stranger deaths have resulted from accidental discharge.

Moving toward the front of the bus may have been a good idea, merely to reduce the likelihood of such an incident, but I didn't want to offend him. I didn't want a confrontation with a man like him, and I didn't want to become another muh'fucka who, for whatever reason, was going to get it.

I sat nervously in my seat and watched him twirling for the better part of half an hour—roughly the time it takes the bus to crawl across North Dallas from the Galleria to Forest Lane Station, at which point everyone else, including myself, disembarked, and he, now alone with the driver, stayed on board, twirling the gun, presumably reciting the same obscure threats.

I didn't really grow up around guns, especially handguns. It's basically impossible to legally own a handgun in Canada. You have to go through an impossibly labyrinthine background check and then get a graduate degree in ballistics or something ridiculous like that, and even those who are successful can only remove their weapons from a locked safe once they arrive at the premises of a licensed firing range. There's no such thing as open carry, and there's certainly no law enshrining the right to bring guns on public transit as there is in Texas.

So perhaps my unease can be chalked up to cultural differences, at least in part. Perhaps I'm a queasy foreigner who lacks a true appreciation for the gun culture that is so deeply engrained in the Texan ethos. Everyone in this state owns a gun, and thus the presence of guns is a familiar feature of life in a way that it isn't in the rest of the developed world. It's a cultural phenomenon that, I will openly admit, strikes me as alien and absurd.

But that's not what put me on edge. There's nothing intrinsically nerve-racking about guns. Second Amendment warriors always talk about how "guns don't kill people; people kill people," and while the way that line is delivered often seems grating and juvenile, it's also true. Guns alone don't kill people, obviously.

No, I was worried because the man on the bus seemed volatile. He seemed imminently threatening. Unlike the 2A douchebags with their "COME AND TAKE IT" T-shirts and Gadsden flag truck decals, I felt like this guy was actually poised to shoot someone. I would have believed it if someone told me that he *had* shot people in the past. I felt unsafe around him, an anxiety reflective of how most middle- and upper-class people—the sort who overwhelmingly avoid riding public transit—would also feel in my position.

Most Dallasites feel that DART is unsafe, just as most Americans elsewhere feel that their public transit is unsafe.

Is the feeling justified? Well, it's certainly understandable.

Many of the people on DART look threatening. They look battered and disarranged. They look like people who have been hit hard by life and who are more than willing to hit back, irrespective of the repercussions. They look like hazards, and most Americans view them as such: hazards that have been inextricably woven within the fabric of the urban spaces they go to such painstaking lengths to avoid.

Some people develop these negative impressions because they actually spend time riding transit, walking around, and witnessing the ongoing dysfunction of urban life. This can't be a very large percentage of the population, however. The American flâneur is a rare creature and certainly a declining one. In a city like Dallas, people who can afford to limit their time in public spaces instinctively choose to do so. So it's not that their fear arises from any meaningful or sustained exposure. Rather, it's that they have intuitions about the city that are contoured by grisly anecdotes and the lurid reporting of the news media.

There are too many cases to list exhaustively, but a small sample of incidents is worth highlighting:

In February 2018, witnesses aboard a train stopped at Pearl Street Station say that they observed one rider advising another rider that his pants were sagging too much. Upon hearing this, the man with the sagging pants, nineteen-year-old Travonte Martin, pulled out a handgun and shot the complainant twice before promptly fleeing the train.

In October 2018, a young, unidentified man in a hoodie approached a stranger at Walnut Hill/Denton Station and asked if he could borrow the stranger's vape. When the stranger refused, the young man proceeded to punch him in the face and steal his phone.

After a dispute between aboard a train at Deep Ellum Station in December 2019, a nineteen-year-old man, since identified as Terrell Pree, shot thirty-four-year-old Chris Washington in the head multiple times. Washington bled out while Pree fled the scene.

In April 2020, thirty-one-year-old Ramon Thomas Villagomez hijacked a DART bus. In the Dallas suburb of Richardson, Villagomez boarded the bus while carrying a handgun and began shooting, which resulted in several shattered windows. Villagomez then forced the DART driver to lead police on a chase that passed through Garland, into Rowlett, then into Rockwall, and finally back to Rowlett. During the pursuit, officers exchanged gunfire with Villagomez, who had fired shots from inside the bus. A Garland officer and a DART officer were shot, and a Rowlett officer sustained injuries after his window was shot out. Eventually, the chase ended on the President George Bush Turnpike when officers used a spike strip to disable the bus. All of this took place while a warrant was out for Villagomez's arrest on charges of aggravated assault with a deadly weapon.

Between these cases and any number of similar incidents in the recent past, violence aboard DART provides local outlets with a reliable stream of startling leads.

Now, targeted attacks are one thing. Given the level of criminal activity in Dallas, it's only reasonable to expect an ambient volume of violence on or around DART property. But when random passengers become entangled, when innocent bystanders are threatened, stabbed, shot at, and killed by complete strangers, as they occasionally are, the public dispenses any notion that transit is a usable service. Whether these fears are rooted in a realistic calculation of danger is largely inconsequential. The effect is that people of means avoid transit.

Again, this phenomenon is exceptionally striking in Dallas, but there are few cities in America that haven't struggled with violent crimes and the viral headlines they tend to generate. Thousands of people become victims on America's transit systems every day, and while only a small fraction of these cases receive national or even local coverage, those that blow up on social media do more than enough to cement the issue in the public consciousness. Though the starchy and moralistic may struggle to admit it, our voyeuristic urge is an itch that must be scratched. Accordingly, any newsman worth his salt adheres to the golden rule of journalism: If it bleeds, it leads.

But just how much violence *really does* take place on American public transit?

Given the degree of underreporting, it's difficult to estimate how likely someone is to be robbed or assaulted, but homicide figures are incredibly reliable, and they're worth considering to contextualize the aforementioned paranoia.

According to the Bureau of Transportation Statistics, only seventeen homicides took place on American public transit in 2019.[6] The likelihood of being murdered on the train really is incomprehensibly small; around three times as many Americans die from lightning strikes in the average year. Compare these numbers to the number of deaths caused by motor vehicle collisions: 36,096 in 2019.[7] Even when the number of deaths caused by public transit accidents is added to the number of homicide victims in public transit, the figure pales in comparison to the number of people who die in their own vehicles. Americans are still about one-thirtieth as likely to be killed riding buses and trains as they are riding in private vehicles.[8]

But perceptions aren't married to (or even influenced by) the statistics. Even in the COVID era, wherein the drastic decrease in middle-class commuters has led to a spike in crime rates, riding transit was much safer than getting into a personal automobile.

Americans don't particularly care. To most people, statistics like these are abstractions. There's something intangible yet definitively scarier about getting mugged, raped, stabbed, or shot on transit than there is about getting mangled in a car accident. People grow up in cars. They spend thousands of hours in cars, zigging and zagging among forty-ton semi-trailer-trucks through lanes of free-flowing traffic, and so the omnipresent danger of the activity becomes difficult to truly appreciate in real time. Whereas when an affluent suburbanite first steps on a city bus or train and becomes trapped in a steel tube with people who have face tattoos, they need no reminder of their vulnerability.

Cynicism and distrust of urban space are the natural corollaries of being reminded, over and over again, that the streets are flooded with violent felons, zombified junkies, and an alarming volume to whom both descriptions apply.

People are reminded by the elevated pedways that link the city's skyscrapers, ensuring that the professional never stoops to the level of pedestrian. They are reminded when their wives, daughters, sisters, and mothers ask to be walked to their cars so as not to endure the few hundred feet of sidewalk, parking lot, or parkade alone. And they are reminded whenever the local news reports on the latest instance of senseless and gruesome violence on their city's public transit.

They are reminded that their world is most safely navigated in the personal automobile, and that out there in the city, in that eternally daunting void between car and building, the world is a ruthless place.

But being in it isn't all that bad. When you're really and truly in it, riding the trains and buses consistently, even the most proximal injustices tend to pass as drab and uninteresting.

In the winter, I was arriving at Forest Lane station on the 486 when I noticed a couple of DART Police cruisers parked adjacent to the bus transfer lanes. It was around 5:00 p.m., so I figured that the officers were on site as part of some rush-hour patrol initiative, despite the fact that even at peak hours DART never reaches half its capacity and, as I hope to have made clear, the efficacy of the police presence is doubtful at best. At worst, it's definitively useless.

There was a fat, middle-aged officer who was holding a radio and sitting in the driver's seat of his cruiser, the door halfway open and the window rolled down. He seemed to be looking for something, glancing left to right as he surveyed the parking lot. He labored less than his partner, who was only slightly slimmer and slightly less middle-aged but whose posture made him seem exponentially more authoritative. The partner was fifteen odd yards from the cruiser, pacing toward the large concrete pillars that elevate the train platform above Cottonwood Creek. It seemed to me that the threadbare structures of the creek-side homeless encampment had caught his attention. He was glancing around, and he was close enough that I could see the stupefied look he wore. Even behind the blacked-out, oversized Oakleys that covered most of his face, it was clear that he was confused for some reason or another. He walked in a circle on the bit of pavement between the bus lane and the platform stairs, muttered something into the radio attached to his vest, and then started back toward the cruiser.

At the time, I remember speculating about the reasons for the call. Maybe one of the local addicts had exposed himself to an especially sensitive passerby. Maybe the officers had been dispatched to break up a fight or check on a suspicious vehicle that was spotted in the station parking lot. Maybe they were just acting busy to kill time like any other hourly employee. All of these theories seemed reasonably likely. I probably spent two minutes hypothesizing, which is really not that much time given how mundane a commute through north Dallas can be.

Then I climbed the stairs of the platform and waited for my train, and the police faded from my mind. It didn't matter to me.

The next morning, as I rode the Green Line on my way to work, I was scrolling through Twitter when I learned what the officers had been looking for.

"Police find woman's body in creek behind Forest Lane DART station"[9]

It turns out they were there for the corpse, which was face down in the water. Someone must have stumbled upon it earlier that day.

I wondered what was left. I wondered how long she had been there, wasting away and waiting to be found. The water in that area is never fast. It's certainly not fast enough to render one unrecognizable in a matter of hours. But it is water. And water enters sponges and changes their composition. Corpses are not so different from sponges. I thought about how she was now nothing more than a sponge and how her digits might be pruning, and how the internal post-mortem occurrences might have caused her to bloat, and how that dark, disgusting fluid might be spilling from her airways, and how the skin around her face might be loosened and slipping and making her look terrifying. She could have been there for days or even weeks. For the officers' sake, I hoped it was a matter of hours, or months, and I felt glad for them that the expiry had occurred in the cool of January rather than the sweltering heat and humidity of a Texas July.

And as I read the article, I thought about her more and more. Her profile and particulars, which were not provided in the article, became interesting to me. My mind wandered. Questions and postulations entered and puttered around in my imagination.

Who was she? How did she die?

Maybe she was a well-adjusted, middle-class suburbanite with a legitimate job and a nice house in a good neighborhood with a sense of propriety and respectable ambitions, someone who just had been looking for a convenient mode of transport around the city. Maybe she was making her way downtown for something casual and unremarkable, like a dinner or a movie. Maybe she had been waiting for a southbound train when she was confronted by someone implacable who could tell by her trappings and comportment that she had things worth taking. And maybe she put up a struggle rather than surrendering her purse immediately. And maybe this angered the assailant so much that he (it was probably a he) decided the easiest person to rob was someone who is dead, and so he shot her or stabbed her and then took her valuables and dumped her lifeless body in the creek before making off. Forest Lane is not a busy station; it is conceivable that all of this could happen without being seen. And anyway, the people who do tend to be around the station aren't the sort of people who are keen on attracting the attention of the police. So maybe this is what had occurred just shortly before I had arrived, and now maybe her family and friends and colleagues were looking for her and worrying, categorically unaware that her life was over because she made the poor, fatal decision to ride the train and risk an encounter with a heartless felon.

But I knew better than that. As someone who actually rides these sorts of buses and trains, shoulder-to-shoulder with the sorts of people who fill them up, I doubted that this is what happened. The woman I just described does not take the train, and she absolutely does not get murdered while taking the train. Ten thousand to one, Jane Doe was a completely opposite woman, a disaster, someone whose death would come as no surprise to those with the faintest awareness of her circumstance.

I bet that she was from the dirty little tent camp just to the south east of the station. Through a canopy of draping oak trees that edges the platform, you can see the mismatched medley of tarps that shelter the area's homeless and provide an arena for their various drudgeries and distractions. By this point, I've probably spent entire days' worth of time taking in their debauchery while waiting for the train. The people who live in the camp and who often venture up the platform stairs and onto the train are very sick and very poorly behaved. They are people who drink nauseating volumes of alcohol through all hours of the day and even more so through the night. They pop pills. They use heroin and crack, and meth, often in plain sight, as nonchalantly as if they were chewing gum. They are drugged up, with nowhere else to go and nothing to do. Predictable dysfunction ensues: noise pollution, public defecation, nudity, harassment of passersby, fighting, rape, and indeed, every so often, murder.

So I assume that the unfortunate woman whom the unfortunate officers discovered must have come from the camp. Maybe she was murdered. Maybe she had simply been using nearby, ventured off on an intoxicated stroll, overdosed, and fell face first into the water. Of course, this could—and probably should—also be considered murder, but who among us has the time or resolve to trace such injustices back to a shameless dealer, an unscrupulous physician, or this country's incestuous rat king of politicos and pharma executives? How many deaths can be laid at the feet of the Sacklers and the officials who enabled them?

As of the time this book was published, Dallas Police had no information about her identity.

What happened was likely a consequence of drug use, or sex work, or organized crime, or petty crime, or some nebulous and unholy blend of them all. It's tragic, obviously, but it's not what springs into the minds of bourgeois readers who, thanks to their entrenched preconceptions about the safety of DART, avoid transit like the plague. As far as they're concerned, random women are being killed in cold blood for the simple act of taking the train. When a city's public transit system serves the additional functions of a homeless shelter, psych ward, brothel, fight club, and drug den, well-adjusted citizens stay in their cars, even when, despite an overwhelming belief to the contrary, the car option isn't safer. It is more comfortable and correctly perceived as more respectable. It maintains a self-assuring degree of separation between normal people and the underclass.

Whether Dallasites are justified in not riding their city's trains and buses, whether they are right to be fearful, really doesn't matter. What matters is that they are fearful. And how could they not be fearful given the impression of their city's public transit gained through media coverage. In May 2022, the *Dallas Morning News* ran this headline:

> *Harassment, drug use and robberies on rise at DART trains and stations:*
> *Riders who use public transit daily are concerned about the increase.*

It's the sort of headline that reifies the deeply entrenched aversion to DART of the newspapers overwhelmingly middle- and upper-middle-class readership. Those mysterious trains and buses? They're somehow managing to become even more lawless!

The article cuts to the chase:

> Incidents involving harassment, violence and lack of safety at DART stations and buses have increased in the last months, leading to concerns among residents who rely on public transit daily.

> From January to March 2022, 428 incidents were reported, according to Dallas Area Rapid Transit data.
>
> The data is compiled into two categories: National Incident-Based Reporting System (NIBRS) and arrests, each divided into train stations and bus stops.
>
> From January to March 2022, 235 NIBRS occurrences and 153 arrests were reported for train stations. For buses and bus stops, 20 NIBRS occurrences and 20 arrests were reported. And in April, two people died at two DART stations. An arrest was made in one of the slayings—an incident that occurred April 30 at the Cedars station.
>
> In comparison, during the same months of 2021, a total 351 incidents and arrests were reported at train stations and bus stops.

What follows in the article is a collection of vignettes from regular riders who have grown increasingly distressed by the danger and disorder aboard DART.

"Every day, it gets worse," fifty-year-old restaurant worker Alberto Espinoza is quoted as saying. "More people are smoking, getting high on the train, or trying to start a fight.... I'm afraid of taking my cell out—what if I get robbed? Many homeless people are always riding the train and sometimes turn aggressive."

"There was a guy who was going over asking people for money," reported Esther Strong. "And then he came to me, and I said, 'No, thank you.' He started yelling and screaming at me, calling me derogatory names. He followed me down the street for like two blocks. No one was there to help, no cops, anything."

Kristen Reagan told the *Morning News* that she now carries a knife aboard DART after having her breasts fondled at Blue Line Ledbetter Station.

"All kinds of these incidents had happened to me in DART," said Reagan, thirty-two. "The police never do anything. So we stop using DART after 6 p.m."

This is a characteristically damning news story about the state of safety on DART. The story documents quarterly increases in crime that are indeed significant and that, unsurprisingly, culminated in a troubling annual increase. Throughout all of 2022, there were 2,783 NIBRS incidents and arrests documented by DART Police, up from 1,765 the previous year.

But even if these articles were ten times as damning and even if the statistical increase they referenced were ten times as high, Dallasites would still be exponentially safer on public transit than they are in their cars.

Again, at the risk of shortchanging reality, the statistics don't matter. Stories matter. What's the saying? One death is a tragedy; one million deaths is a statistic? It's true. Perceptions matter. Psychology matters.

Phenomenologically, there is a sense of safety and control people have in their private vehicles that they don't have when they're at the mercy of whoever else is on the train or bus—a sense of safety and control that profoundly circumscribes the demographics of the DART ridership.

CHAPTER 7

The Women of DART

IT WAS 6 A.M. IN northwest Dallas. The signs and neon lights above the miles of strip mall storefronts were dimming as the sun rose. Short, unshaven men in shoddy clothes lined the curbs, sipping coffee and smoking cigarettes as they waited to be picked up in trucks and hauled out to cash-paying construction sites. Some of them smiled and laughed as they talked, but it seemed feigned and superficial. It would have been feigned and superficial were I in their position. The aptly named mockingbirds were derisive and loud—loud enough to be heard over the sound of the engine whenever the bus came to a stop. They were jeering and making fun of those who had to live and work somewhere so ugly. Everything was as it was: monotonous, soulless, and industrially an emic. It was and is the type of place that breeds misanthropy. Nobody wanted to be there. At least, I didn't want to be there.

Maybe the people sitting behind me wanted to be there.

"Not here, baby. I won't do it here."

She had a frazzled, sandpaper voice courtesy of the menthol Newports in her spindly hand, or so I assume. A long, olive-colored army jacket covered most of her frame, which was gaunt and which was a very common frame among the women who ride DART. It fit her as more of a cape or a cloak, and that seemed quite deliberate on her part.

"Why not? We're at the back. Here's fine. You'll do it here."

He, likewise, was not an impressive man—mid-thirties, if I had to guess. He had skinny limbs and a thick, pudgy torso. Dark jeans with raised, oversized stitching covered his legs. I couldn't tell for certain, but they seemed like they were Ed Hardy. Maybe they were Ed Hardy-adjacent. They looked too cheap and obnoxious to be expensive, and he looked too poor, but that's probably a sign that they were. Up top, he wore a graphic T-shirt with an eagle, wings spread, beak open, talons out. His face was asymmetrical, and his eyes were sunken in. He looked like a cast member of Jersey Shore who had just been woken up from a long coma.

"Don't worry about it. I'll give you more when we get there. Just do it here, bitch."

They had got on one stop after me and decided, for whatever reason, to take up the seats immediately behind me. This early in the morning, there were only four of us on board: them, the driver, and myself. Between their conversation, I could hear the sound of them kissing in the sort of tangled, sloppy way one might expect from drunken teenagers at a house party.

"What if the driver sees, and, like, freaks out?"

"He won't and he won't," said the man, who was right on both accounts. Apparently whether I would see or freak out was not important. It's possible that they meant to use me as an impromptu screen to block the driver's line of sight. But the man was right: the driver wouldn't have cared.

Then there was a lot of movement and friction. There was more kissing, and I could hear the sound of hands on denim and the eagle bumping up against the army jacket.

"Just do it here, bitch. You'll do it here, okay?"

"Baby, I'll just do it when we get there. Why can't I just do it when we get there?"

"You can just do it here." He sounded more insistent now. "You'll do it here."

"Okay, fine, baby, I'll do it here." She sounded reticent but not upset.

And then there was a brief pause before the kissing noises resumed, and so did the rubbing of fabric, albeit much less forcefully.

"You know I like you, right?" she offered.

"Just do it. Stop fuckin' playing. Just go. I gave you some already and I'll give you more when we get there."

Whether he was referring to drugs or cash wasn't clear, but their entanglement was unambiguously transactional. And then I heard a zipper. And I could hear what sounded vaguely like the sound of sloppy kissing, but that I knew was something else.

Against my better judgment, I dimmed my phone and used the screen as a periscope to see what was happening through the gap between the seats. I suppose I already knew what was happening, but I felt inclined to confirm. It felt necessary to do so that I would know I wasn't going crazy and that what was going on behind me actually was going on. Maybe that makes me a voyeur, but I don't think it does. I think the impulse was normal given the setting.

And it turns out I was right. I wasn't going crazy. Her head was thrust in his lap at 6:00 a.m. on a city bus.

I read an article a few years ago about a young couple in Indonesia who were flogged for engaging in some sort of nondescript PDA. Apparently, that's a fairly normal course of justice in Indonesia. The couple in question lived in an especially fundamentalist province of the nation where Sharia law is strictly enforced, and I distinctly remember that the article used the term "canoodling" to explain what the criminals were engaged in. I got the impression that it was first base at the very most. Maybe things were getting handsy. "Canoodling" is an ambiguous term, but I don't believe it refers to anything overtly sexual, certainly nothing penetrative. In any case, I remembered the article because it seemed bizarre to me that a government in a part of the world that faces so many cataclysmic problems would be devoting such energy toward something as benign as cuddling. To anyone with Western moral sensibilities, it's clearly an outsized, almost evil response. On the other hand, Western tolerance and permissiveness do create the sort of brutish libertines who make a mockery of public space, the sort who were now rounding third less than a yard behind me. And as I sat there on the 486, I wondered what punishment would be delivered to these people if we were all on a bus in Indonesia and I was pious enough to report them. Maybe they would be stoned or hung from a crane or something like that.

"You know, I could have just left you on this bus if you didn't do it," he said to her, "How would you have liked that?" It was still in her mouth when this was asked.

She lifted her head and smiled, revealing several gaps where most people have teeth.

"Baby … Stop."

"Yup. Could have done it. I could have just gotten off at the next stop and left you here all on your own. Now wouldn't that have been fun?"

"Baby, stop. That's not funny," she said playfully. She was still smiling and clearly believed that he was joking. And he probably was joking. Yet there was an understanding between them that such an abandonment on his part really would have been bad for her, or that it would have been unprincipled in some obvious way.

I couldn't tell if he was her boyfriend, or a John, or some strange combination of both. I was, however, certain that he was a man, and that she found his presence reassuring. Despite his discourtesy and abrasiveness, he was important for her to have around. She was reassured by the fact that he represented a barrier of protection against the lechers and reprobates that are so frequently aboard the vehicles of DART, or so the thinking goes. This was the not-so-subtle implication.

She would have been fine by herself, but she had clearly determined it was worth performing the act that she was performing in order to retain the protection of this crude, doughy man.

I thought about this a great deal. This woman had clearly been through a lot in her life. I'm guessing she had spent many nights sleeping on the street, negotiated with far too many men like the man behind me, and generally faced far crueler tribulations than most Americans will in a lifetime, and still, she was bothered by the notion of riding transit alone. She looked to be a tremendously hardened, desensitized woman, but being on DART without a man was something she viewed as threatening.

Most of the women I know feel this way about transit. They don't feel safe. They are anxious about who they will encounter when they are waiting at the bus stop, or on the platform, or while they are riding, or while they are walking to or from transit itself. In some sense, this is strange given the fact that women are much less likely than men to be assaulted basically anywhere in public, including on transit. But again, crime rates are tough to internalize. Women feel powerless and assailable, and ultimately, that's much more important than any statistic.

It isn't just Dallas or Texas where women are put off by public transit. In one study done by New York University's Rudin Center for Transportation, 75 percent of female respondents reported experiencing some form of harassment or theft while riding public transit, and 88 percent of those who have experienced harassment did not report the incident to authorities. [10]

Like all of the social ills examined in this book, however, the problem strikes me as especially pronounced in Dallas.

A 2018 article in *D Magazine* offers an interesting glimpse of the angst and apprehension that female DART riders (rare as they may be) have been forced to accept as normal.

"The Woman's Guide to Surviving DART: When embarking on Dallas public transit, every ride brings its own peril and pervs." It's a blunt headline, but it's hardly an exaggeration.

Written by a woman who claims to ride the train daily, the piece provides a list of suggestions for dealing with the sort of uncouth men one inevitably meets while riding DART. Some of the author's recommendations are fairly damning:

> Be prepared to get off your train at the wrong stop.
>
> The train arrived. The large man followed me onto the car. Maybe it was just his train. Maybe he was following me. Maybe he would follow me off the train, too. Maybe nobody else would be there when I got off, in the bleak, inhospitable landscape of the Walnut Hill DART station—except for him. In that case, I will hope he is an evangelist, which is a thing I have never hoped about anyone before. This is why you must always be prepared to get off at the wrong stop. It's not just about avoiding the ones who will leer at you, talk to you, ask what you're doing all alone. It's not just about the ones who will slowly, quietly reach out from behind you on the train and touch your hair. A man once followed me onto the platform at Walnut Hill Station, across an island of dirt and through some bushes, to a shadowy street crossing and along a sidewalk, quickening his pace, as I broke into a run and finally had to jump into traffic to

lose him. Is there any better system for a creep to track a woman than her daily train commute?

Do not accept drugs.

Strangers will offer you drugs, especially at the West Transfer Center and West End Station. It's not like *The Wire*; people aren't palming Double Cheese or Election Day. It's usually more like: "Do you want drugs?" Because a direct question deserves a direct answer, I respond with a polite "No, thanks."

Respect your bus driver.

One night, late, there was a crazy person on the bus. He got violent. The driver called the police. I sat on my bus seat, crouched like a cat. The police interrogated the man. Then the police interrogated the driver. Then the police interrogated me. It was a whole big interrogation thing.

The police handled it well. It was not like other times when I have seen them standing over a prostrate body in the middle of the West Transfer Center. My bus driver is always afraid. Ever since the July 7 shooting, he told me, he is afraid of every passenger who gets on his bus carrying a backpack, who might have a gun. "Anyone on this bus might be a serial killer," he told me, looking around.

And like their prosecution notices conspicuously posted on their trains and buses, DART's own public messaging is also fairly damning. In conjunction with a range of advisories to be on the lookout for loiterers and the disorderly, DART's "Passenger Guide to Safety and Security" directs riders to do the following:

> First and foremost—be aware of your surroundings and those around you. It is easy to tune everything out while on your phone or listening to music. This is a prime opportunity for criminals to take advantage of the situation. Victims and witnesses are not able to assist in identifications because they did not know their surroundings.
>
> "The situation" in question being a passenger who is minding their own business rather than actively serving as a deputized officer for DART Police.
>
> Keep valuable items out of sight. Most crimes are based on opportunity. By having valuable items out of sight, including cell phones and MP3 devices, you don't make it easy for the criminal to quickly grab whatever they see and run off with it.
>
> It's worth noting that the "opportunity" in question is seen as a consequence of rider behavior rather than organizational policy …. Using your phone on the train? Don't be ridiculous!
>
> Keep your personal items under your control at all times. Items such as purses, packages, and brief cases set down even for "just a second," are an easy target for a snatch-and-run.
>
> Like a running back, the onus is on you to make sure your head is up and your grip is firm.

Accordingly, there are not very many women who ride DART, and those who do ride out of necessity. This must be true basically everywhere outside of a handful of cities like New York, Chicago, and DC—and even in these anomalies, it's clear that passenger safety is a major barrier to increasing ridership, particularly among women.

It's a shame because women are much less likely than men to own cars, so it should theoretically be easier to push them toward adopting transit. Though without the mass presence of socialized, high-functioning men, the type whose presence neutralizes public venues like movie theaters and shopping malls, women don't want to ride transit. And socialized, high-functioning men don't ride public transit. They take their cars. So a hapless Catch-22 exists, and people stay in their lanes, so to speak.

Women are scared because transit is messy in this city and in this country. While it's unlikely they will ever be assaulted or seriously harmed, a paranoia exists because of the frequency with which some women are leered at and harassed. Why is this the case? They are leered at and harassed so frequently because their fellow riders are largely broken, intoxicated men with nothing to lose. And why is *this* the case? Their fellow riders are broken, intoxicated men with nothing to lose because transit systems have evolved to serve many unintended functions, as previously described, one of which is sheltering broken, intoxicated men with nothing to lose.

If they can find any other way to get around, women will take it. And who are the women who can't? They are women with serious, intractable problems. They are, generally speaking, the homeless, the prostitutes, the addicts, the disabled, and the working poor. They are the women of DART, a profoundly unlucky group that gets from point to point alongside sad, broken men who will often force them to suck dick in the backseats of buses.

CHAPTER 8

No Scrubs

"LISTEN, MAN, IT REALLY ISN'T my business, but I haven't seen your car in the lot lately."

He looked more solemn than he would for a normal water-cooler conversation. "I can… You know … give you a lift to work until you get things sorted out."

I didn't really know what he meant.

"I had a buddy in college who got caught … well … uhhh … he had an incident…. I know it can really screw your life up for a while," he added.

"I'm not quite sure I know what you're talking about."

"Like I said, it's none of my business," he said, leaning toward me and lowering his voice, "but it's more common than you'd think. I don't mind giving you a ride in the meantime."

I raised an eyebrow and didn't say anything.

"It's just that I've seen you at the bus stop these past few weeks. It looks miserable. You really don't have to do that. You're a young guy and I totally get it if you slipped up and did something stupid. Let me help you out."

And then I understood what he was getting at. As must have been true of many of my colleagues, he assumed that the only reason I would have been riding public transit was because of a DUI. My honest, well-intentioned coworker took for granted that the only possible reason why I, someone who is clearly middle class, would be taking public transit rather than my car was because I was legally barred from operating a motor vehicle. In hindsight, I guess that's a fairly reasonable theory, but it's also one which few Americans seem to challenge or lament. That there was any other explanation for why I was riding public transit was totally out of the question, a reality which underscores America's absurd cultural obsession with the automobile.

The irony of the matter is that even if I had been charged and convicted of a DUI, I would quite likely have been able to acquire an "occupational license," sometimes referred to as a "hardship license," in order that my ability to drive to work not be affected. God bless Texas. Even when people use their vehicles to commit the potentially fatal offense of driving under the influence, our legal institutions afford criminals the grace and flexibility requisite to spare them from having to set foot on buses and trains. That sort of punishment would be humiliating and depraved. Need there be any reminding? These are the same legal institutions that allow for 23/1 solitary confinement and capital punishment. But I suppose some sentences go a bridge too far.

In America, the ability to own and operate an automobile is not seen as a mere privilege borne of economic expansion; it's seen as a foundational aspect of personal liberty. As has been expounded by the philosopher Loren Lomasky, among many others, the ability to travel whenever, wherever, and with whomever one wishes has yielded profoundly liberating effects that can be felt throughout society:

> Automobility is, by definition, promoted by the automobile. The complementary nature of autonomy and the automobile is only slightly less evident. Being a self-mover in the latter part of the twentieth century is, to a significant extent, being a motorist. Because we have cars to drive we can, more than any other people in history, choose where we will live, where we will work, and separate these two choices from each other. We are more able to avail ourselves of near and distant pleasures and to do so at a schedule tailored to individual preference. We are less constrained in our choice of friends and associates by accidents of geography. Our ability to experience an extended immediate environment is notably enhanced. The automobile is, arguably, rivaled only by the printing press (and perhaps within a few more years by the microchip) as an autonomy-enhancing contrivance of technology.[11]

Indeed, since the 1920s, the automobile has been synonymous with freedom. With the invention and commercialization of the Model T, Henry Ford emancipated Americans from their static condition and set them up for a century of unfettered access to anywhere that's paved, and even many places that aren't. In some sense, this newfound ability allowed for individuals to feel more self-determined and self-actualized, as though their agency was safeguarded from government encroachment. These sentiments flourished in predictable ways during the Red Scares of the ensuing decades. It should therefore come as no surprise that Ford consistently jostles for position with presidents, founding fathers, and civil rights icons whenever lists of the greatest Americans are compiled. We think of driving as a precious, inalienable dimension of American life, and as Ford was the first to make this experience accessible to the masses, he has ascended to a sort of saintly standing in the national consciousness.

It's tough to be quintessentially American without a vehicle. It's tough to live the quintessential American dream or have quintessentially American experiences. And so we have become vehicle obsessed.

This fixation is evinced in all facets of society. Hollywood would not be what it is today without car culture. Ferris and Cameron, for example, wouldn't have been able to play hooky with Sloane if they had to take the L train. No Cubs game, no "Twist and Shout," no Art Institute. They needed the Ferrari 250. Marty McFly and Doc needed the DeLorean. Would the people behind *The Fast and the Furious* be able to make a billion dollars from what is essentially the same film ten times in a row if the country were not so infatuated? The examples go on and on. Would James Dean still be the fabled sex-symbol he is today if he had died from heart disease rather than in the crumpled driver's seat of a Porsche 550 Spyder? Michigan Stadium, the largest athletic field in the Western Hemisphere, can seat up to 107,000 fans; that's less than half the capacity of the Indianapolis Motor Speedway at 257,000. You could fit two Michigan Stadiums worth of fans in the Speedway and still have room for two Madison Square Gardens. It's literally just a circle that the cars go around 200 times in succession, but 257,000 line up to get in. Car culture is magnetic and ubiquitous. It is, in that vein, an effective instrument of politics, which is why Democrats and Republicans alike bend over backwards to be seen as champions of the industry and of the culture more broadly. It's why veritable city-slickers, born and raised New Yorkers like Trump, will posture about their fondness for the Ford Raptor during manufacturing plant speeches and why a geriatric like Biden, someone who obviously should not be operating a vehicle, will release ads of himself flat-shifting in a vintage Corvette. You have to look and act the part if you want to lead a nation of drivers, man.

While it is true that the adulation toward the automobile transcends party lines, the role of the automobile in American life is particularly resonant among the American right. There is a certain breed of American conservative whose disposition toward the car is so closely intertwined with his conception of personal freedom as to verge on parody. This person believes that the intrepid spirit and undaunted restlessness of the Pilgrims and Westward expansionists live on in their own moral fabric, which is why they, unlike their indolent European cousins, need to drive. To varying degrees—in some cases consciously and in others subconsciously—they believe driving is a biological necessity, almost a matter of genetics. They contend in earnest that vehicle ownership ensures freedom of movement and association just as gun ownership ensures the ability to resist tyrannical governments. There is a predictable relationship between per-capita gun ownership and car ownership at the state level. Montana and Wyoming, two of the reddest states in the union, top the charts in both categories. New York, surprise, surprise, is at the bottom.

Yet the socially conservative defense of personal vehicles as a cultural fixture of American life is just one piece of the puzzle. There is also a breed of libertarian for whom the attraction to the automobile is not only that it serves as a vessel in which to navigate the world as a boundless individual but also that it reduces tax burdens by diminishing the size and scope of government. At least insofar as governments might otherwise allocate resources toward the development of public transit infrastructure like rail and bus networks, these people are happy to support a system that shifts the financial responsibility for transportation onto private citizens. After all, America is a playground for the rugged individual, and if you want to make it here, you can't expect Uncle Sam to be your chauffeur. Just as healthcare, housing, food, and any other consumer good or service are the responsibility of the individual, so too should we treat transportation. Or so the thinking goes.

It turns out the American love of driving exists without a corresponding admission that building roads is expensive.

Americans with libertarian impulses (i.e., Americans) recoil at the prospect of a government intervention that would increase the cost of driving for the individual motorist. When Secretary of Transportation Pete Buttigieg suggested that the gas tax may need to be pegged to inflation in order to fund the Biden administration's $2-trillion infrastructure plan, he was lambasted by all but the staunchest tree-huggers and cycling buffs. As it became clearer and clearer just how poorly the proposal was received by the American people, the White House forced him to walk back the suggestion on cable television and also to ensure that his related proposal of implementing a "miles-driven" tax would not see the light of day. That this was the result of his perfectly sensible suggestion speaks to the fervent delusion of the American people. The federal gasoline tax, which currently stands at 18.4 cents per gallon, has not been increased since 1993. If the rate had been pegged to inflation like a standard proportional tax, it would be generating 33 cents per gallon, nearly twice as much revenue as it does today. Even when state excise taxes are taken into account, the average American is only paying around 56 cents per gallon for gasoline, a mere quarter of the OECD average and only a sixth as much as the Dutch.[12] It is therefore little wonder why the federal government's Highway Trust Fund, an account that draws its revenue from fuel taxes and finances the construction and upkeep of roads, racks up massive deficits and perpetually struggles to remain solvent. Nobody wants to admit how expensive it is to build and maintain infrastructure that can sustain a culture where everyone thinks their travel must be done in a private vehicle.

Car culture promotes an individualistic, laissez-faire outlook that is obviously flawed, and it's not just the nominal cost of driving that matters. It's not just about the ostensible price of purchasing a car or gas, or even roads, or the ostensible tax savings when public transit goes unfunded. Substantial externalities to driving exist, and those impact everyone, especially people who are priced out of car ownership entirely. Car culture is an iceberg, and these costs are just the tip.

When thinking about the true cost of car culture, one must consider how much is paid for through the police who patrol the highways, the firemen who must fight mangled frames with the jaws of life, and the paramedics who ferry victims around to emergency rooms. Obviously, all of these people need cars of their own that need gas, insurance, and servicing. But the knock-on effects on public health and safety must be confronted, as well. Besides all of the unquantifiably tragic fatalities, how many people are dealt unrecoverable injuries in car accidents? What are the costs to society of these accidents? How much are the surgeries? The physiotherapists? The ramps? In the same way that calculating the price-tag of a foreign war is more complicated than tabulating nominal expenditures like weapons and salaries, you cannot simply add the superficial costs of car culture to assess the impact of cars on our culture. There are countless effects that the average American may go their entire life without considering. A 2014 study from the National Highway Traffic Safety Administration concluded that the economic impact of vehicle collisions amounts to $871 billion in a single year.[13] To put things in perspective, that's about a fifth of the entire federal budget, more than double the amount of all combined state and federal infrastructure spending.

It's difficult to truly grasp just how thoroughly the repercussions of driving percolate throughout all levels and sectors of the economy. And it's troubling to follow the money, but it's important in order to understand which industries rely on maintaining the status quo. If you start pulling the threads, you realize that there are a lot of people whose jobs would disappear in a world without car accidents. Academics at the Pacific Institute for Research and Evaluation have broken down the impact of crashes into ten major categories:

Public services: fire and emergency medical services (EMS) at the crash scene, incident management services, police services, coroner or medical examiner services for fatalities, vocational rehabilitation and social services to the injured and their families.

Medical care: emergency department, hospital, physician's office, rehabilitation, mental health, nursing home, and pharmaceutical services for injury victims. Government shares in these costs through Medicare, Medicaid, and other public medical insurance programs, as well as limited direct service delivery (e.g., medical care at community health centers and Veteran's Administration hospitals).

Foregone taxes: income and sales taxes not paid because the injured have less income and the dead are lost to the workforce.

Social safety net expenses: social services and public assistance payments including Social Security Disability Income, welfare (Temporary Assistance to Needy Families), food stamps, housing assistance, low-income home energy assistance, and other programs that assist people when injury leaves them permanently disabled or indigent.

Adjudication and sanctioning: costs of processing crash-related citations, plus costs of incarceration and lesser sanctions, and costs of license point tracking and license suspension. Unfortunately, nationally representative data were not available on these costs or the portion of them paid by offenders.

Fringe benefits for government employees and their benefit-eligible dependents: sick leave, private health, disability, and life insurance payments, and for employees injured on the job, Workers' Compensation insurance payments.

Administrative costs when government employees are injured or killed: co-worker distraction, hiring and training temporary or permanent replacement workers or paying co-workers overtime to fill in, loss of unique skills, processing personnel changes, processing sick leave and workers' compensation claims.

Incident investigation and liability expenses: costs incurred when government employees are involved in crashes while working include investigation and record-keeping on crashes, for-cause drug and alcohol testing, and disciplinary action. If the government employee is at fault (i.e., causes the crash), the government also is liable for the losses of anyone who was injured or whose property was damaged in the crash.

Court costs: court costs associated with liability lawsuits against government and its employees.

Property damage: including damage to roadside furniture and government vehicles.[14]

There are the above costs, which are in some ways indirectly borne or otherwise abstract, but cars are incredibly straining on personal finances as well in ways that are concrete and consequential to the layman's budget. Especially among the bottom half of American households, those whose income is below $70,000, the attachment to cars is one that can totally eliminate opportunities for upward mobility. Even in a place like Texas that does not collect a state income tax, this median sum of $70,000 would only leave $56,000 in take-home pay. According to AAA, the average annual cost of vehicle ownership is $9,561 once insurance, maintenance, depreciation, and other operating expenses are aggregated. So to participate in car culture, even with only a single vehicle, this median household pays nearly a fifth of their take-home pay. More likely, the household has two cars; they're probably spending closer to $20,000 a year. It's tough to overstate just how much wealth creation average Americans lose out on because of this highway robbery. If the hypothetical household were free to invest, say $15,000 a year in an index fund with a 6 percent average annual yield, they would be able to save more than a half million dollars over the course of the next twenty years and almost a million over the course of the next thirty years. Far from these figures, the median American household has a net worth of just $104,000.

Despite the state of Texas not having an especially high number of vehicles per capita by American standards (0.78), Dallasites are extremely reliant on cars. According to figures from the 2020 US Census American Community Survey, Dallas has the highest number of vehicles per household (1.91) and the highest percentage of households with access to a vehicle (95.4 percent) of America's top ten largest cities.[15]

Maybe those who find themselves comfortably within the ranks of the middle class can manage to maintain a tolerable lifestyle while running on the treadmill of car ownership. Maybe they can toss away a quarter of their income while continuing to sustain themselves. And maybe they can even do this while slowly putting money into savings or some sort of appreciating asset. For many Americans, however, the squandering of wealth demanded by car culture produces abiding debt and destitution.

Overall, American consumer auto debt totals 1.37 trillion dollars, an incredibly disproportionate amount of which belongs to Texans. According to 2019 data from the credit reporting agency Experian, twenty-four out of twenty-five of the cities with the highest levels of auto debt in the country are located in Texas. Midlanders owed an average of $33,847 per resident. The consequences of this debt are especially grave for the working poor, the demographic with the lowest credit scores and those who are most likely to be harmed by predatory lending practices.[16]

Typical Rates, Payments, and Interest for a $20,000 Auto Loan Repaid Over 6 Years[17]

FICO Score Range	Average APR	Monthly Payment	Total Interest Paid	Total Cost
781–850	3.50%	$308	$2,202	$22,202
661–780	4.50%	$317	$2,858	$22,858
601–660	7.50%	$346	$4,898	$24,898
501–600	12.00%	$391	$8,152	$28,152
300–500	15.00%	$423	$10,449	$30,449

It's a huge problem. Forty percent of Americans have a FICO score below 700, and 28 percent have a score below 650. What this means in practice is that the poorest members of our society, people who feel just as much of an obligation to partake in car culture as the middle and upper classes, often end up paying tens of thousands of dollars more for their vehicles than the wealthy.[18] This is why most dealerships make a lot more money through interest payments than they do through sales margins. It's not about selling cars; it's about sucking blood. It's also why the archetype of the car salesman as a sleazy, worthless leech is so recognizable to the average person: most car salesmen are, in fact, paid to be sleazy, worthless leeches. By and large, the industry is a racket that capitalizes on the witless, although not unjustifiable, insistence of members of the working class that they need a car to survive. If you're an American who can find a way to own a car, chances are you'll do it, even if it tanks your personal finances. The alternative is taking public transit, and that's simply out of the question for so many people.

Car culture is here to stay, at least for the foreseeable future. It will continue to exist not only because of how it has affixed itself within the American economy and not only because of how many people rely on cars either directly or indirectly for their paycheck or dividends but also because the predominant social force that props it up is so pervasive and durable: sex.

The principal reasons why Americans do not ride trains and buses are not the same for men and women. For women, as per the previous chapter, it is reasonable to perceive transit as unsafe. It's not that public transit really is unsafe or even more unsafe for women than for men, but that doesn't matter. Perceptions are, I repeat, far more consequential than reality. Women don't feel comfortable on transit, so they don't ride it. If this nation's transit systems were not so dirty and chaotic, maybe they would.

What's keeping men from abandoning their vehicles for transit is not a perception but a reality. For American men, it's almost impossible to enter or maintain a relationship without owning a car. Unless you live in one of the nation's few downtown cores that has good public transit infrastructure and an impossibly high cost of parking, not owning a car is something that most women find supremely off-putting and, usually, disqualifying. American women view car ownership as a very basic marker of wealth and self-sufficiency, and, in most cases, it is. In most cases, American men who don't own cars are exceptionally poor or ineffectual or seriously lacking in some other domain. If you don't have a car, it's because you can't afford a car. And in a country where basically anyone can get financing for a car, you have to be a real loser to be an exception. This is how people think. And the heuristic exists because it has quite a bit of substance. Those who deviate from the norm by not having a car are self-evidently unfit for relationships. It is because of this entrenched feminine proclivity that men are so motivated to stay in the driver's seat.

This is true for men, regardless of their relationship status. For single men, driving a car is a way to show a woman that you are able to do the bare minimum to play the courtship game. It is the prerequisite that shows you can pick her up and take her places—that you are, on some rudimentary level, mature and capable of self-determination. This perspective is so obviously ubiquitous that it's difficult to find anyone who wasted their time conducting a survey to collect quantitative data, but female-directed relationship columns illustrate the sentiment quite clearly. From *She's Single* magazine:

> Not only is his inability to drive unattractive, it actually can indicate other potential relationship deficiencies such as commitment issues, lack of responsibility, and even low self-esteem. If he can't even commit to owning and maintaining the upkeep of a vehicle, what makes you think he's ready to commit to you? Your relationship is not like paying off a monthly car payment, but it does require upkeep. If he can't put in the effort here as a functioning adult, he won't be able to in the relationship either. [19]

From *Bolde:*

> A man's confidence is generally linked to him knowing who he is, what he's doing with his life, and his feelings for you. Not having something as basic as his own car and no plans to get one shows a complete lack of motivation and confidence. In other words, it's not a great idea. [20]

From *The Standard*:

> If you are a man and you are well past your teens and still do not have wheels, you don't deserve a woman, or sex for that matter. In fact, you should give up dating altogether, until you get your $#!£ together and buy a car.... I'm sorry if I sound a little brash, but when I see a man taking the bus I don't automatically assume

> that he is on the bus because he is slowly but surely working his way up to CEO or saving for school or whatever. To me, he is an irresponsible bum who does not know how to work hard and smart, because if he did, he would not be taking the damn bus.[21]

Of course, for single men, car ownership also serves as an opportunity to stand out in a crowded dating market. It's no surprise that 99 percent of people who own Ferraris also own a penis.

Even if they are able to efficiently get around by taking the train or bus, most married men or relationship guys would never dream of giving up their vehicle. The reason they wouldn't dream of it is not because they have some sort of constitutive devotion to their shitty Toyota Corolla but because of how it would make them look in the eyes of their wives and girlfriends. Not owning a car as a grown man would go beyond the pale. It would be emasculating. It would be humiliating and intolerable, obviously.

Basically, everything a man does is in pursuit of impressing a woman (either real or imagined) or in pursuit of staying in the good graces of whichever one he has managed to settle down with. Men are cowardly, and their relationships with women and cars are in equal parts oppressive and absurd. For all the talk and exploration of toxic masculinity in this culture, very few people recognize that one of its most crippling manifestations is the pressure men feel to own a car, a pressure wholly justified given the priorities of women.

> *And no, I don't want no scrub*
> *A scrub is a guy that can't get no love from me*
> *Hanging out the passenger side*
> *Of his best friend's ride*
> *Trying to holla at me*

Most American women know exactly what TLC was talking about and are vicariously contemptuous of the scrub in question. It's a song that is deeply American, one that reflects a psychological attribute unshakable for so many of the nation's women.

No, no, no, no
If you don't have a car and you're walking
Oh yeah son, I'm talking to you

Men and women both appreciate the importance of male car ownership on a fundamental level. That being the case, sixteenth birthdays are a much more momentous occasion for adolescent males than for adolescent females. Getting your license and no longer being dependent on your parents to go out and about is liberating in a way that is difficult to overstate.

For normal, red-blooded American guys anyway (those who get their licenses the instant they're allowed to), sixteen is when a boy becomes a man. Your stock in the market immediately increases by an order of magnitude, and I am quite certain that if you were to plot out the average age of sexual firsts for American teenage boys, there would be a striking cluster of data points in the weeks or even days subsequent to the sixteenth birthday. Given that cars are such a dominant aspect of life in the United States, sixteen is a far more meaningful age of majority than eighteen or twenty-one, at least for guys.

And this is all just the way it works in this country, and in this city and state especially. You turn sixteen, buy a car, and then spend as much time and money as is necessary to make sure you stay on the road, lest you be pegged as some sort of unseemly leper who takes the filthy, lunatic-infested public transit system. It goes unquestioned that an automobile is required to live a normal, well-adjusted life and, more importantly, to be a normal, well-adjusted person.

For all of the obvious societal ills this system produces, Americans seem pathologically incapable of reckoning with its costs or reimagining something more closely aligned with Asian and European countries.

Car culture is terrible, and we should resent that it has become such a defining feature of American life. It is the product of a social mythology that is reified by corporate interests and that rests largely on feminine avarice and masculine hubris. We all think we need cars, and that makes some people fabulously wealthy while forcing others into unrecoverable debt.

Car culture is expensive and injurious, but far more importantly, it abases the human experience. It atomizes us and makes us sick, fat, and unproductive. Paradoxically, it reduces our mobility by turning our cities into a labyrinth of impassable parking lots and freeways. Car culture makes our cities ugly. It pushes us to accept the monstrous lie that the material realities of urban life cannot be beautiful, that development must first and foremost accommodate cars. Apparently, we have to live in concrete hellscapes. Apparently, that's just how things have to be.

CHAPTER 9

Eight Million Inmates

ON ONE OF MY MORNING commutes, I almost saw a man commit suicide. It was February 2 , just after 6 a.m. I was riding the 409 from East Dallas to Southwestern Medical District Station. The driver was a plump, tired-looking man with dull eyes and a scraggly beard who didn't even pretend to look at my proof of payment when I boarded. I quite like these drivers, and, luckily for me, they constitute the overwhelming majority. There's something more authentic and admirable about them than the few who smile and feign concern about whether or not you bought a ticket. Being a bus driver must be terrible, and having to perform this work while enforcing pointless rules must make it that much worse.

The sun was still not up when we turned from Lemon onto Haskell, and the arterial streets were mostly empty. Though as we approached the I-75 overpass, I could see the flashing lights of three or four squad cars through the bus's windshield. For whatever reason, the police were blocking the freeway's northbound merging lane. This seemed odd to me at first because, as far as I could tell, no accident had occurred. I didn't see any shattered glass, or mangled doors, or any other sign that a wreck had recently been cleared. Then the bus got closer, and I saw that a few of the officers were out of their vehicles, standing on the curb, looking toward the guard rail. On the ledge, I saw the silhouette of a man dressed in ill-fitting clothes.

The police cruisers had created a bottleneck for the few vehicles that were, like us, trying to cross the interstate into Uptown. As a result, we moved very slowly past the man and the officers, who were, by all appearances, trying to coax him away from the ledge. The bus stopped quite close to him, maybe a few vehicle lengths away. I would have been able to see the details of his face if he had turned around. I was also near enough now to see that the police had closed down traffic below by creating a barricade. The man was just standing there. Twenty feet below him, cars, pickups, and semis would have barreled by just moments earlier. Some must have been going sixty miles per hour.

I tried to think about whether or not a twenty-foot drop would be enough to kill him. I have always found these sorts of things hard to intuit. Twenty feet is about the height of a third-story balcony. It probably wouldn't be enough to kill him, I thought to myself. The impact would probably just shatter his legs and maybe a few vertebrae. More likely, he had planned on timing a jump so that he would hit the ground an instant before being hit by the grill of a vehicle. That would be the sensible way to do it if, in fact, he really did want to do it. The suicide attempts of men are much more likely to be fatal than women, so I thought that he probably did genuinely want to do it. Pavement, car, death. No prolonged anguish. The strategy reminded me of the stories you hear every so often about people who, after poisoning themselves, put a bullet through their head, lest either method be unsuccessful on its own.

As I sat there on the 409 looking at the man who was standing very still with his hands at his sides and his chin glued to his collarbone, I wondered what he was thinking. I wondered why he wanted to kill himself. There are, of course, many reasons why people attempt suicide: the death of a loved one, the dissolution of a romantic partnership, financial hardship, loss of employment, religious estrangement, philosophical introspection, and countless other afflictions.

But, then again, there's rarely a single, all-encompassing cause. People attempt suicide because they no longer wish to exist in the world. This sentiment can be chalked up as a consequence of negative changes in familial or social life, or the degradation of spirituality, or ontological shock, but it can also be chalked up as a consequence of the physical world. That is to say, there are many metaphysical reasons why someone might become fatally depressed or nihilistic, but it's also the case that many people are suicidal, at least in part because the physical world around them *proposes* fatal depression and nihilism.

Maybe the man on the ledge had just learned that his wife was cheating on him. Maybe he had just lost his job. Maybe the bank was repossessing his house or car. Maybe he had just been diagnosed with a terminal disease. Maybe he had an upcoming court date for an unbeatable charge. Maybe he had spent years battling an addiction that finally became too much to bear. Any or all of these might be true.

What is also true, however, is that Dallas, as a physical place, pushes people toward the edge. I can't help but suspect that the cityscape had something to do with why this man was in the position that he was in. People don't want to continue living when they're living in a place that isn't worth living in. To an appallingly greater extent than is reflected by the design and form of the cities in which most Americans live, our psychology hinges on our environment.

In its form and design, Dallas is a very normal American city: dull, desolate, and demoralizing. No well-travel ed Dallasite would ever contest this. Unfortunately, Dallasites tend not to be well-travel ed, so the dullness and desolation are seldom acknowledged or criticized.

I do like the downtown core, however. The architecture of the city's downtown core is interesting. Gothic revival buildings like the Kirby stand immediately next to those in the neoclassical style, like the Adolphus Hotel. Fifty-five-story postmodern skyscrapers like the Chase Building are built next door to beautiful mid-nineteenth-century churches like the Cathedral Santuario de Guadalupe. The Spanish baroque-style Majestic Theatre neighbors the Moderne, Art Deco clocktower of the Merc. The distinctive red sandstone bricks of the Richardson Romanesque Dallas County Courthouse shares Dealey Plaza with the less ornate but much more famous Texas School Book Depository. To be sure, there are buildings downtown that are beautiful and stimulating. Moreover, they are strikingly diverse, and this diversity feels coherent and reflective of the diversity that has become so definitional of modern American life. I really do enjoy walking around in the downtown core. Whenever I have an opportunity to do so, I like to meander the streets with my headphones in and admire what people have built. The experience is inspiring and humbling. More people—normal people, not just homeless people—should do this. It would be good for them, and it would be good for the downtown core.

But Dallas is not its downtown core. The downtown core is a tiny plot of land just slightly over a square mile in area within a Metroplex that is nearly 10,000 square miles. The core is a pixel on the screen—a tiny enclave that is circumscribed by a massive ring of interstates. Architecturally, downtown bears little resemblance to the rest of the city. It is wrong to conflate the two and say that Dallas is a city made up of beautiful buildings because there are a handful of beautiful buildings in the core. There are virtually no beautiful buildings outside the core. The neighborhoods that are closer to the core are comprised of rectangular, featureless apartments. Similarly, the outer neighborhoods and suburbs are just oceans of cookie-cutter units, separated by pointless lawns and oversized driveways, lodging insular households that are totally anonymous to their surrounding community. It's all very dehumanizing. It's depressing to look at it from the window of an airplane. At 30,000 feet, you really come to appreciate just how thoroughly the ugliness has sprawled, how steadfastly Americans have distanced themselves from one another.

One of the names for the downtown core is the Downtown Historic District, an apt description. Unintentionally, it reveals the city's regressive, ruinous attitude toward planning and development. The Downtown Historic District is so named because it represents a bygone era, perhaps an imaginary one, in which aesthetic value was not subordinated to narrow economic interests as a matter of course. It is "historic" in that its visual charm and grandeur are unaligned with contemporary priorities.

Ugliness is bad, and it is especially bad when it takes up a lot of space. And it is especially, especially bad when its excessive use of space evolves in harmony with the construction of highways, city streets, and parking lots, which are themselves ugly and demanding of space. Pretty much half of the surface area of Dallas is paved. That's a lot of square miles of pavement. Devoting half of a city's area to vehicle transportation is not only detrimental for the obvious reasons that it prevents homes, theaters, restaurants, parks, gardens, and museums from being built, and it is not only detrimental because it makes these buildings more distant from one another; it is also detrimental because it sequesters the cities into cells, many of which are only accessible by car and many of which are inaccessible entirely.

Though drab and uninteresting, it is easy to walk across a parking lot to get from one point to another. Most streets, likewise, are easy enough to cross, even if a little bit of jaywalking is required. Getting over sixteen lanes of an interstate, however, is incredibly hard, particularly when the lanes exist at different heights and particularly when no controls or overpasses exist to facilitate pedestrian travel. Two points could be a hundred yards apart as the crow flies, but they may be hours apart by foot. The Metroplex is a labyrinthine grid of interstates, so the result is thousands of cells that are, just like the disjointed, cookie-cutter houses of suburbia, separated in a way that proscribes social interaction. Dallas, like all American cities, is an aggregation of cells. In some sense, these cells make them like prisons.

In a way, our cities may even be worse than prisons. I worked in a prison when I was younger. It was a dismal place. Just looking at the cells made me claustrophobic, and I imagine that living in one would be hell. But they were cells, and cells keep people apart. That's what cells are for. They exist for the express purposes of containment and segregation. It is very simple and easy to appreciate this teleology in the context of prisons.

Yet the prison's cells had doors. While the inmates were, as inmates tend to be, confined to their cells for the vast majority of the day, daily opportunities existed for programming and social activities. They were allowed out to eat together and to exercise together and to play board games and to watch movies and to attend group counselling sessions and to do many other activities that are fundamentally social. The fraudsters, arsonists, rapists, and murderers were all allowed to assemble for such things because in the context of the prison, it is understood that solitary confinement is depraved and inhumane. Unlike the cells created by our vehicle-centric cities that are checkered by thoroughfares and highways, the cells in prisons are impermanent. They only exist insofar as the jailors keep the doors locked. But in the American city, we have confined ourselves indefinitely. There is neither a key to be turned nor a barred door to be swung open. There are no external jailors to emancipate us from the tangled web of concrete for the interludes of physical unity and interaction that keep humans sane.

It's worth noting that not all prisoners are afforded regular time outside of their cell. Of course, in some prisons, there are people who are confined to their cells for days, weeks, months, or even years at a time without exposure to other humans. These people suffer serious and indelible psychological effects that correlate highly with self-harm and suicide, which is why cells used for solitary confinement are devoid of objects that might be used to end one's life and why the concrete floor and walls are sometimes padded with a benevolent layer of foam. If there were a freeway overpass in every cell of every prisoner who is currently being held in solitary confinement, many of them would get on the ledge.

Dallas would make less people want to jump off an overpass if it had more public spaces. Access to public spaces that host rich, inclusive social gatherings obviously improves mental health and well-being, and it should be seen as an indictment of American culture that such few places exist. The problem is especially critical in Dallas, given its expansiveness and decentralization. Klyde Warren Park, the Main Street Garden Park, and Pacific Plaza, all within the downtown core, are almost always empty because nobody has any way of getting to them. People use public parks when they are within walking distance, and, for Dallasites, walking distance is a few hundred yards at most. Unfortunately, not very many people live within a few hundred yards of these places. Of the nearly 8 million people who live in the Metroplex CSA, around 10,000 people live downtown, and those who do are not inclined to spend time in public spaces. They have access to the private plazas and rooftops of their luxury high-rise apartments. And maybe they enjoy these private spaces, but there is no substitute for vigorous public space that is green, open, and accessible.

The Akard Street square in the AT&T Discovery District is often busy; it's the closest thing this city has to a true public space. And yet, as the name suggests, it is less of a communal square and more of a ritzy outdoor food court, closely surveilled by private security, where monied suburbanites congregate for cocktails and hors d'oeuvres whenever they're in the mood for "a night in the city." The AT&T Discovery District is basically just a place where the upper classes go to LARP as metropolitans. Actually, living in a city does not interest them, but the setting makes for a polished Instagram post.

What happens outside of happy hour and outside the Discovery District? With the exception of homeless people who pass the time drinking and collecting cigarette butts from the pavement, most of the downtown streets are empty. One autumn morning, I walked down Pacific Avenue for four blocks, from Pearl to Akard, without seeing a single person. I walked half a mile in the middle of one of the biggest cities in the country without seeing a single person. How is that possible? There's no other country in the world where that could happen. It was like being the sole survivor in an apocalyptic sci-fi. It wasn't even that early, and it's not as if Dallas was under any lockdown. The sun was up, and the few cafes and restaurants that exist in that area had their signs turned on. But the streets were empty. What I should have seen were old men sipping coffee and playing chess. I should have seen a weathered guitarist in bohemian garb, busking for spare change. I should have seen joggers jogging. I should have seen painters painting. I should have seen college kids collecting signatures for some useless petition. I should have seen a woman reading outside a cafe, and I should have seen a man approaching her, pretending he knows and likes the book for the sake of an introduction. I should have seen people out and about, interacting with one another like real human beings. If this isn't happening in the nucleus of the city, it isn't happening.

The best part about living in Montreal is the parks. My apartment was in the Plateau, just off Mont-Royal and St. Laurent, which put me within walking distance of some of the nicest parks on the continent. Lahaie, Wilfred-Laurier, Lafontaine, Mount Royal, Square Saint-Louis, and Jeanne-Mance were all nearby, and any one of them would be the nicest park in the city if it were to exist in Dallas. Sometimes I would spend entire days in the park, walking around and listening to music and being a living, breathing constituent part of the city. And I enjoyed it very much because there were nice people to talk to and nice things to look at, and in many ways the parks felt more inviting and comfortable than my own home. Montreal's parks are beautiful. They are heavily speckled with tall oak and maple trees that provide a sense of intimacy, but not to the point of darkness or suffocation. They have interesting features like fountains, ponds, amphitheaters, gazebos, pools, and they are integrated into the rest of the city in a way that makes visiting them seamless and organic. Montreal's parks are not sequestered by freeways or parking lots; they are the central feature of dense residential neighborhoods. While it is only twice as large an area as the downtown core of Dallas (again, home to 10,000), more than 100,000 people live in the Plateau, most of whom do not own vehicles.

It isn't just about design or location. Parks are only as valuable as people perceive them to be. They are not valuable if they are ignored or unutilized. People need to love and respect parks for them to be good parks. The appeal of Montreal's parks is largely a cultural phenomenon. It is largely a result of the fondness Montrealers have for congregating in beautiful public spaces. Whereas Dallasites view and use parks as incidental features of the neighborhood that are necessary and useful only insofar as little leaguers need a place to play ball and dogs need a place to relieve themselves, Montrealers view parks as one of the foremost venues for social life. The latter appreciate "going to the park" as a standalone activity. It is a normal thing that people of all ethnicities and social classes will do in Montreal. Old people go to the park. Young people go to the park. Rich people go to the park. Poor people go to the park. Everyone goes to the park.

Few parks exemplify this cohesion as well as Mont-Royal. During the warm months, thousands of people will congregate every day to lay out their blankets and sit on the park's grassy slope overlooking the city. They will drink wine and listen to music. They will sunbathe and read magazines. They will slackline and smoke weed. They will talk among their cliques, but they will also approach people who they do not know and amalgamate into larger social groups. They will be real human beings in the real world, and they will do the things that real human beings are meant to do.

Every Sunday, Mont-Royal becomes the site of a festival called Tam-Tams. Around the base of the 100-foot-tall monument to Sir George-Étienne Cartier, Montrealers from all walks of life gather to partake in a massive, decentralized drumming circle. From sunrise to sunset, an army of people, unknown to one another, sit in a big circle and beat their drums, usually bongos. People will come and go as the day passes by, and certain leaders will sometimes establish patterns and cadences, but the drumming never stops. It's quite the spectacle. It is moving and evocative. Connections to personal identities feel unimportant around the Tam-Tams drumming circle because of how transfixing the music and general atmosphere become. At Tam-Tams, everyone is a human. If only for a short while, people transcend their demographic descriptors and revert to a primal stage where they are just banging away on a bongo and immersing themselves in the raw energy of the music and their fellow humans, unconcerned about the tasks and tribulations of modern life.

The park is Montreal's heart, and Tam-Tams is her heartbeat. These things invigorate the city and make its denizens healthier and fulfilled. They bring the homeless shoulder-to-shoulder with doctors and lawyers. They bring liberals shoulder-to-shoulder with conservatives. They bring descendants of the nation's founding stock shoulder-to-shoulder with its most recent immigrants. They engender profound human bonds and make people happy. Dallas doesn't have anything like this. It has a critical lack of public space and, consequently, a critical lack of public events. As a result, Dallasites do not know one another or see one another. They are strangers, imprisoned in a gnarled web of concrete.

With 14.5 out of 100,000 Americans killing themselves every year, the United States has a significantly higher suicide rate than the rest of the developed world. The rate is 9.7 in France, 6.9 in the UK, 5.3 in Spain, 4.3 in Italy, and 3.6 in Greece.[22]

In addition to having urban green spaces that are much more accessible, European cities tend to have green spaces that occupy a much larger proportion of urban areas.[23]

Countless academic and governmental studies have documented the myriad somatic and psychological benefits associated with access to green space, but the World Health Organization's "Urban Green Spaces and Health" is arguably the most rigorous and comprehensive amalgamation of research. Within this ninety-three-page report,[24] the authors present evidence that exposure to green space is associated with reductions in chronic stress (using hair cortisol as a biomarker); reductions in neural activity in the subgenual prefrontal cortex, which can alleviate the symptoms of depression; and a range of similar psychological benefits as reported by participants in a variety of international studies.

Another study from researchers out of UC San Diego found that people who live near parks and green spaces are 44 percent less likely to have a diagnosed anxiety disorder.[25]

To be sure, there is overwhelming evidence that access to green space is a key determinant of mental health.

It would be far too reductive to attribute something as complex as suicide to a handful of variables like exposure to urban greenspace. The United States has way more firearms, for example, than any of its European cousins. And yet, just as it would be absurd to overlook all of the shotguns, rifles, and revolvers that avail themselves to Americans experiencing suicidal ideation, so would it be absurd to overlook the features of European cities that demonstrably enhance their populations' mental health: the sprawling parks, plazas, and public squares that are interwoven with the more "pragmatic" elements of urban design.

Had he spent the previous day in a beautiful park like Mont-Royal or banging away on a bongo at a gathering like Tam-Tams, I do not think the man would have been standing on the ledge of the I-75 overpass. I think he would feel more human and more enthusiastic about his own potential for a redeeming future. I do not think he would be interested in ending things early.

CHAPTER 10

A Very Big Problem

"I DON'T TRUST IT. WHY'D IT take so quick for 'em to make it? God knows what's in it. I think they might be experimentin' on us. I sure as hell wouldn't take it if they offered it to me today."

"I might. I bet they'll make us get it at some point. They'll force us to get it. That type of thing always happens with the government."

"Nah, not me. I ain't on no type of conspiracy shit, but I don't trust it. I'll let other people get tested on first. I ain't tryn'a let it be me who's gettin' tested on. Nah, I won't sign up even when I can."

"I hear you. I hear you."

The two women then sat in silence for a moment. The fence-sitter was clearly hedging her language so as not to inflame things with the other. Then the less skeptical one spoke.

"I do know of some people who have already gotten it. Technically, they're already letting some people get it, if they fall into a … ummm … into a certain category."

"You talkin' healthcare workers? I don't see why they don't just keep the masks on and whatnot."

"Healthcare workers, but I also heard they was booking appointments for old people and people who have some type of *underlying condition*." She said these last words very slowly and made sure they were accompanied by air quotes so as not to come off as too solidly allied with the prevailing institutional wisdom.

"Underlying conditions?" the skeptic replied. "What'chu talm' bout some underlying conditions?" the air quotes being repeated, incredulously.

"Well, I mean falling into one of their categories. One of my girlfriends was telling me about it. Technically, I think I would be able to get an appointment now if I wanted to."

"Whatchu' mean? What's wrong with you? You got some type of disease?"

"No.... Not a disease or anything like that. *Technically...*" she said the word "technically" very slowly and then repeated it. "Technically, I think I count as being overweight or having a high body mass or something. You know how it is. And *technically*, I think that means I qualify as having an underlying condition."

"What? Girl, you curvy, but that ain't no disease. That's normal." She laughed. "Fuck a technically."

"Amen, amen."

This was part of a conversation I overheard in January, riding the Green Line during Phase 1B of the vaccine rollout, a time in which Texans older than sixty-five and adults with at least one chronic medical condition were eligible for vaccination. Both of the women were DART fare-enforcement officers, dressed in big, navy blue khakis and agency jackets adorned with the little service shields that, at least in theory, convey their authority to any members of the public who might be otherwise unconvinced. They were sitting in the seats immediately in front of me. Actually, that isn't quite true. Only one woman was sitting in the seats immediately in front of me. Her colleague was sitting in the row of seats across the aisle, kitty-corner to me. I pluralize "seat" here because there is absolutely no way that either of them would fit in a single seat, and even with two seats, there was considerable overflow.

These women were nearly identical in height and weight, as far as I could tell: 5' 6", give or take an inch, and approximately 300 pounds. Despite looking rather new, a noticeable bulge appeared in the midsole of their shoes, as if a pneumatic press had been used to crush the heel. Behind their masks, I could tell that they were breathing from their mouths, tired from the activity of sitting upright and talking. They were both the sort of people who, had they been alive 150 years ago, would have been able to make money as freak attractions in a traveling circus. And yet in this modern context, it seemed totally inconceivable, at least to one of them, that their weight was in any way dangerous or aberrant. They were content to regard the CDC's diagnostic categories as a mere technicality, something trivial and unimportant, in the same way a tomato is technically a fruit. It would be pedantic, in their mind, to place any real import on the characterization.

I've noticed this delusion and overheard similar exchanges in many other places: at work, at the grocery store, in airports, in cafes, in restaurants … wherever large numbers of Americans exist. And I have noticed and overheard them among a sweeping range of demographic groups. Americans who are pathologically fat have a bizarre tendency of telling themselves that they aren't, and it's rare that they receive pushback. Clearly, this is the result of an evolving cultural standard.

In my grandparent's era, it was totally acceptable to casually make fun of fat people. To an extent, it was acceptable to malign and denigrate them. Corporate advertisements and government PSAs from the twentieth century would explicitly message that being fat was unhealthy. Moreover, they would emphasize and warn about the social reverberations of being fat. Fat men were portrayed as listless dopes, and fat women were portrayed as boorish and unfit for affection. And this is how such people were publicly perceived. Back then, institutional messaging was unequivocal in telling people that mockery and ridicule are the just and natural consequences of being overweight and that one must do whatever is necessary to maintain a healthy figure.

In some ways, it is good that our society has evolved to become more compromising and sensitive. It is good that people aren't being encouraged to smoke cigarettes in order to curb their appetites and stay trim. Maybe it is good that fat people no longer need to worry about being jabbed and prodded for an attribute that is, in some ways, superficial and unimportant. But, then again, this attitudinal evolution has in large part created a country where nearly everyone has a disease, one which is serious and life-threatening, not merely "technical."

Three out of every four American adults are overweight, meaning that their body mass index is greater than or equal to 25. For reference, the average American man is 5' 9", meaning that he falls into this category above 170 pounds. The average American woman is 5' 4", meaning that she falls into this category above 145 pounds.

Somehow it seems more concerning to consider the inverse: that one in four Americans does not fit into this category. One in four Americans has a normal, healthy BMI.

I can't go to the grocery store without seeing someone who weighs twice as much as they should. I can't go to the mall without seeing someone in a non-ambulatory scooter. It's crazy to me that this is just a normal thing. Is there any other medical condition that afflicts 75 percent of the population? I can't think of one. The average American woman now weighs as much as the average American man did in 1960, and this is just seen as a normal thing that isn't truly worth talking about or solving. If that weren't bad enough, people don't even think of it as a disease. We've all just become accustomed to the present condition. We've normalized it, and we pretend it isn't a problem.

But it obviously is a problem. It's obviously a very big problem. It is an epidemic, and it is by far this country's leading cause of death. Overweight and obesity-related illnesses like heart disease, cancer, and diabetes are so much more deadly than anything else. It's not even close. It is a problem that kills millions of Americans every year and one that costs the US healthcare system $173 billion every year.[26] This is obviously the biggest problem in the country.

The problem is not only killing people, it makes them unproductive.

Obesity can have a significant impact on the workplace, not only in terms of employee health but also in terms of productivity, absenteeism being the principal issue. Research has shown that obese employees are more likely to miss work due to health issues related to their weight, such as diabetes, heart disease, and joint problems, which leads to costs for employers in terms of lost productivity, sick leave, and healthcare expenses. In addition to absenteeism, obesity can also contribute to presenteeism, which is when employees are at work but are not performing at their full capacity due to health problems.[27] Obese employees are more likely to experience fatigue, difficulty concentrating, and reduced mobility, which can all impact their ability to perform their job duties effectively.

The economic consequences of obesity and overweight are starkly evinced by the predicament the American military currently finds itself in, a predicament that would shock and horrify people in a normal, functional country. Thirty-one percent of youth (aged seventeen to twenty-four) are too heavy to even be considered for service, a number that is steeply on the upward trend.[28] Policing and firefighting must be facing similar challenges. All labor-intensive jobs, for that matter, must be increasingly threatened by America's seemingly unstoppable bulking. Hopefully, automation outpaces gluttony. Exoskeleton technology better hurry up.

Leaving aside economic concerns, fat people aren't fully alive when they're fat. Carrying all the fat around makes them immobilized and lethargic. Relative to healthy people, fat people are less inclined to go to pools or to go out dancing or to play Frisbee with their kids or to go for bike rides. Fat people don't like walking places, and that makes it very challenging for them to live in a city like Dallas without owning a car. Problems beget problems. Dysfunction begets dysfunction. Driving everywhere creates a more sedentary lifestyle, which only exacerbates the weight problem. Then everything in the city has to be built around cars because everyone is too fat to walk anywhere, and this forces a tragic, downward spiral of obesity and ugly, concrete cities.

Riding DART is hard for fat people because there is significantly more walking required than there is when travelling by car. Sometimes, taking transit even requires climbing stairs. Cityplace Uptown Station demonstrates what I mean. In order to get from the underground platform to street level, you need to do one of three things. If they are moving, you can ride the escalators, although they are often not moving—often, they are just stairs. Or you can take the service elevator, although the service elevator is often occupied by a homeless person who is covered in their own vomit and urine and likely to be drunk and disagreeable. Or you can take the regular stairs, always an option, although there are exactly 209 of them, and that's asking a lot for some people.

Public transit is not designed for fat people, and, in turn, fat people don't like riding public transit. Fat people like driving in cars, which is often a big reason for why they're fat in the first place. The interconnection of fatness, car culture, low transit adoption, ugly cities, and depression is a vile compound that's difficult to separate or solve. All the phenomena penetrate one another and inevitably compound to make life miserable.

Were it not for examples abroad, the American situation might be less disturbing. The epidemic of obesity, however, is just that: an epidemic. It is not global or universal. It is not a pandemic. There are countries in the world where most people weigh a normal amount, and where it is highly unusual to see someone who is severely overweight or obese. In the wake of the COVID-19 crisis, reflecting on the experience of healthier countries is revealing and worthwhile.

America's handling of the COVID-19 crisis has been assiduously criticized by some of the country's most influential voices. "Fumbled" and "bungled" became the terms of choice in the editorial pages of *The New York Times, The Washington Post,* and *The Atlantic*, among others. Our outlets of record decided that the United States dropped the ball, and, thanks to them, it is now received wisdom among all but a small minority that our pandemic response is cause for humiliation.

It is difficult to assess the relative response of the United States given international disparities in human development and testing prevalence, but one thing is certain: our per-capita fatality rate is among the worst in the world. According to Johns Hopkins, the US case fatality rate is 1.1 percent. In South Korea it's 0.1 percent.[29]

Why is this? Why have Americans been over ten times more likely to die than South Koreans? Obesity is the obvious answer. Obesity is the strongest comorbidity for fatal cases of COVID-19. Medical authorities dispute a great deal about COVID-19, but they don't dispute this. All else being equal, your risk of death increases with your weight.

One study published in the *British Medical Journal* analyzed mortality data from Johns Hopkins University and the WHO Global Health Observatory data on obesity. Of the 2.5 million COVID-19 deaths under consideration, 2.2 million were in countries where a majority of the population is classified as overweight, defined as a body mass index higher than 25. Compiling data from over 160 countries, the report found linear correlations between a country's COVID-19 mortality and the percentage of overweight adults.

"There is not a single example of a country with less than 40% of the population overweight that has high death rates (over 10 per 100 000)," the report said. "Similarly, no country with a death rate over 100 per 100 000 had less than 50% of their population overweight. Vietnam, for example, had the lowest death rate from Covid-19 in the world (0.04 per 100 000) and the second lowest levels of population overweight at 18.3%."[30]

In some parts of the world, places like Vietnam and, indeed, South Korea, fat people basically don't exist. Everyone is more or less a healthy weight—a weight that would be considered svelte and maybe even waifish by the warped standards of the United States.

One study out of Tufts University found that "92 percent of 364 measured restaurant meals from both large-chain and non-chain (local) restaurants exceeded recommended calorie requirements for a single meal." And these excesses were not marginal by any means. The research team also found that "in 123 restaurants in three cities across America, a single meal serving, without beverages, appetizers, or desserts sometimes exceeded the caloric requirements for an entire day."[31]

Indeed, dietary customs are the most conspicuous explanation for international disparities in obesity rates. Whereas Americans think it's normal to inhale 4,000 calories of ultraprocessed food product, the norm in South Korea is to eat two or three conservatively portioned bento boxes comprising meat, rice, kimchi, and seaweed. South Koreans do not think it's normal to eat an entire Domino's pizza. South Koreans don't consume three days' worth of fat while snacking on buttered popcorn at the movie theater. South Koreans don't make a habit of eating small mountains of nachos before an entrée.

There is no analog of IHOP in South Korea. They would find something like that nauseating. They would find the shapes of the people who stuff themselves into the trough-like booths at IHOP disturbing.

South Koreans have developed a culture that incessantly pressures people to reduce excessive body fat. Euphemisms like "curvy," "thick," and "full-figured" are not conscripted in South Korean parlance to obscure illness. South Koreans don't glamorize and fetishize being overweight. Unlike in America, those who are lean and slightly built are celebrated for their beauty and held up as an aspirational benchmark. K-Pop singers are national idols; their figures are plastered everywhere to remind the masses of the optimal physique. South Koreans are obsessed with their bodies, and while this obsession undoubtedly has its drawbacks and liabilities, their society is clearly better off, all things considered.

Again, mode of transportation is another factor that has to be taken into account when looking at the massive disparity in overweight between the two countries. Far fewer people drive cars in South Korea than in the United States. In Seoul, for instance, 23 percent of people drive a private vehicle to work. In Dallas, 90 percent do. The lifestyles are completely different. South Koreans wake up and eat a small mortar of kelp and bean sprouts before walking to the train station, standing on the train, and walking the rest of the way to work. Americans wake up and then get in their cars before they ritualistically hit a drive-through for a coffee-flavored morning milkshake.

Every so often, the American media roll out a story about a "perfectly healthy" person in their twenties or thirties who died from COVID. Reliably, when a picture of the deceased is put out, the person is hundreds of pounds overweight. They are morbidly obese. Their deaths are as tragic as anyone else's, of course, but it's delusional to pretend that they weren't already diseased. There's no good reason to obfuscate what killed them. COVID-19 killed as many Americans as it did because many Americans were already incredibly sick. South Korea didn't fare as well as it did because they had some sort of brilliant response strategy, like some influential Americans might have us believe. They didn't have a special hand sanitizer or a more sophisticated rapid test. Hundreds of thousands of South Koreans contracted the virus. They weren't better at figuring out which drugs to use, which buildings to close, or when to reopen them. Their people were healthier and therefore very resilient from the outset.[32]

I wonder what would be required to solve the problem in America. What levers would need to be pulled in order to address this overwhelming sickness that has somehow become an acceptable feature of American society? What would need to be done in order for overweight and obesity to be as rare in the United States as it is in South Korea?

When considering these questions, I can't help but think about the response by governments and corporations to COVID-19. These institutions forced the world to stop spinning on its axis. Businesses were forced to shut down. Masks were mandated everywhere except private residences. Schools were forced to send students home. People were not allowed to workout at gyms. The ability to travel abroad was eliminated, and even domestic travel was severely curtailed. Many jurisdictions banned celebrations and religious activities altogether. Curfews were implemented, something that would have seemed unthinkably repressive just a few months earlier given the actual risk to public health. The people in charge decided that we were in a war, and that austere, wartime measures were entirely justified. They decided it was worth moving heaven and earth in order to delay the spread of the virus.

And maybe it was worth it. Some people think the lockdowns were a successful public health policy. But if they were worth it, if public health really is that important as an overarching cultural value, then it must also be worth it to devote equal or greater energy to getting the average American down to a healthy weight.

A proportional response to the weight crisis in America, I suspect, would seem wildly offensive and unacceptable to many Americans. But if politicians and public health officials actually cared about Americans, if they approached obesity and overweight with the same focus and solemnity as they did COVID-19, they would enact substantive policies to encourage people to lose weight. Many people would object to these policies, but they would work.

If our policymakers really wanted to solve the problem, they would impose steep excise taxes on sugary beverages and food products rather than facilitating a system where soft drinks are the most common item acquired by SNAP households,[33] where exclusive beverage contracts are awarded by publicly funded universities to companies like Pepsi and Coca-Cola,[34] and where these same companies are even provided recurring contracts from the United States Department of Defense.[35]

If our policymakers really wanted to solve the problem, they would reallocate farm subsidies to increase the production of meat and specialty crops like fruits, vegetables, and nuts rather than staple commodity crops like corn, wheat, and soy. Corn, the main ingredient in high-fructose corn syrup, is by far the most heavily subsidized crop in the United States, with its farmers having received over $116 billion in subsidies from the United States Department of Agriculture since 1995.[36]

If our policymakers really wanted to solve the problem, they would fund garish ad campaigns to scare people about the health effects of excess body fat—campaigns that are analogous to anti-smoking and anti-drug ads. As one study published in *The New England Journal of Medicine* concluded, "if past obesity trends continue unchecked, the negative effects on the health of the US population will increasingly outweigh the positive effects gained from declining smoking rates.

Failure to address continued increases in obesity could result in an erosion of the pattern of steady gains in health observed since early in the twentieth century."

If our policymakers really wanted to solve the problem, they would force the closure of fast-food restaurants. They would pay to serve organic, calorically suitable meals in school cafeterias. They would install scales out front of buildings and they would render automatic referrals to doctors, dieticians, and personal trainers if the number exceeded a certain threshold. They would impose all of this, if they really cared about people and demonstrated that care with the same fervor and inflexibility that accompanied COVID restrictions throughout the pandemic. If they really cared, they would leverage the full force of the government to bully people into compliance.

All of these policies would be effective. Far more effective than the policies used to deal with COVID.

Given human nature and the everyman's penchant for cold hard cash, it would probably be easier to pay people to keep their BMI below 25. America's average BMI would plummet if the government wrote people checks every month to stay in shape. Money could be sent out in the same way the stimulus checks were sent out. The only thing people would have to do in order to receive the payment is visit a certified government weighing and measuring station and verify their continued eligibility. Governments have created cash lotteries to incentivize COVID vaccination. How is paying people to not be fat any different? Hundreds or perhaps even thousands of dollars per individual could be sent out in this manner every month, and the program would still make sense on purely fiscal grounds given the associated economic savings. The nominal medical costs of treating obesity-related illnesses alone are in the trillions of dollars a year.[37] The true, comprehensive societal costs are incalculable.

Aesthetic considerations, for instance, are incalculable. They should matter. Smoking is unhealthy, but at least it looks cool.

Being fat is both unhealthy and unattractive; there's no offsetting value. I look at pictures of people from decades and centuries past, and everyone is so attractive. They are a size that is healthy, and that health is reflected in the look on their faces and by the activities in which they are engaged. In looking at these pictures through a modern lens, I instinctively note how physically impressive they are, how well-formed and proportioned. They could all be models, I think to myself. Then I remember that those proportions have been the norm for tens of thousands of years, and it's only recently that being doughy and droopy has become the standard.

I didn't write this chapter to moralize or finger-wag. Many of the people I love weigh more than they should. But like so many Americans, they are not healthy. I wish they were healthy. I wish our institutions were genuinely oriented around improving their health. The fact that they are not makes me resentful, and I think cultural and institutional apathy toward something so consequential should breed resentment.

I don't know why more people don't talk about this. It all seems so tragic and obvious.

CHAPTER 11

Below the Bottom

THE GAME STOP SHORT SQUEEZE was widely seen as a clash of economic classes, a battle of David versus Goliath. After decades of ravenous front-running, shorting, and predatory speculation, billionaire Wall Street financiers were finally on the losing side of a battle with the people whose blood they have long made a profession of leeching.

This is how the event was covered in the media anyway, and it's certainly how the event was discussed by the credentialed, middle-class cuspers with whom I tend to hang out. The lads of WallStreetBets sparked a movement among retail traders fueled by an abiding cultural resentment toward the financial elite and a deep sense of class solidarity. The squeeze wasn't merely a technical phenomenon. Something about the movement seemed personal and morally compelling. People with modest brokerage accounts like us were at the bottom, and we were finally getting a chance to stick it to the conniving sons of bitches at the top. That's how it seemed.

Of course, we weren't at the very bottom. Whenever I stepped foot on the train, it was painfully obvious that we weren't even close to the bottom.

I would always try to be productive during my commutes. I would scroll through Twitter, catch up on the news, and, especially during that feverish week in January, I would trade stocks. I traded very actively that week, and I came out with a considerable profit.

When the music stopped and the precarity of the squeezes became obvious—after I had made more money from messing around on a trading app than most DART riders make in a month—I thought about all the drunks walking up and down the aisle, all of the zombified wage slaves staring aimlessly out the window, and all of the anonymous people huddled beneath their dirty blankets. They are the serfs of our neo-feudal age. Clearly, these are the people who are at the real bottom, and I don't think that fact would have been so apparent to me had I not been riding transit. People's perception of the bottom is relative. It's a consequence of their environment. Because the people who write the columns about events like WallStreetBets are unlikely to see, hear from, or spend time around anyone worse off than the typical Robinhood amateur, public discourses on interclass relations exclude vast swaths of the American polity.

None of the people riding DART would have known what I was referring to had I asked them about GameStop. They wouldn't have cared if I told them that Melvin Capital was getting obliterated or that retail brokerages were freezing volatile securities. Revelations like these would be completely meaningless. It would be as if I were speaking to them in Mandarin.

The people on the train have no exposure to the stock market. Accordingly, they have no interest in or understanding of the stock market. Indeed, there are many things that the people on the train relate to with such indifference and ignorance.

The people on DART don't care about the NASDAQ. They don't care about the Oscars. They don't care about presidential debates. They don't care about what's going on in Ukraine. They don't care about interest rates or deficits. They don't care about who's on the masthead of *The New York Times* or who gets invited on Bill Maher.

No.

They care about the Mavericks and the Cowboys. They care about pop music. They care about how much it costs to buy cigarettes. They care about which stores take EBT.

The people who ride DART are not politically or economically oriented in any deep or meaningful sense. Their conceptualization of the world is material and hyperlocal. I don't mean this to sound patronizing or condescending. I'm trying my best to be descriptive, and this sort of myopia is easily understandable given the distressing condition of the American lower class.

These people lead lives that are immensely draining, and just getting through the day often demands all of the resolve and energy that they can muster. They don't have the motivation to engage in the affairs that are engaged in by people who purport to be their benevolent custodians and countrymen. They aren't positioned to be class-conscious.

In fact, the contrary seems to be true. These people are actively encouraged to embrace attributes that are divorced from class, which prevents them from organizing and agitating for meaningful reform. Anyone who looks and sounds like me, anyone who is routinely and breathlessly accused of class reductionism, will know what I mean.

Democrats, as a matter of course, are more focused on extending hollow rhetorical overtures toward specific demographic groups than they are on pursuing concrete solutions to the nation's staggering inequality. All things considered, unfortunately, it's been an effective political strategy. In the 2020 election, 65 percent of Latinos and 87 percent of Blacks went with Biden. When Biden got into office and immediately reversed his promise to send $2,000 stimulus checks to all Americans earning under $75,000, it's not as if the Democrats paid for it with a mass exodus of Black and

Latino voters in 2022. By and large, they stayed with Biden. And in lieu of the desperately needed economic relief they were promised, minorities were rewarded for their loyalty with Kamala Harris, a race-baiting goblin who referred to the Jussie Smollet hoax as "an attempted modern-day lynching." It's very troubling, but political maneuvers like this, empty as they are, seem to be sufficient in the minds of the Democratic powerbrokers.

Why pay for the votes of poor people when fomenting racial resentment is free?

For the past sixty years, Democrats have managed to safeguard their reputation as the default party for the nation's minorities, even if it has meant stoking animus between America's ethnic groups at every possible turn.

Republicans, conversely, are too tightly bound to their private-sector paymasters to earnestly court this grossly underserved segment of the country. The GOP is a party thoroughly and unshakably gripped by corporate interests. It seems constitutionally incapable of adopting a more redistributive politics, no matter how obvious it is that multiracial working-class populism is the party's only lifeline amidst America's rapidly changing demographic landscape.

Some of this bipartisan disregard for the poor is undoubtedly a result of the disparity in political contributions. Nearly a third of Americans making over $150,000 annually report donating to political candidates and parties, whereas only 7 percent of individuals earning less than $30,000 identify as donors.[38] It costs money to win elections, so it should come as no surprise that the interests of the people who have money are privileged over the interests of the people who don't. To put it bluntly, poor people have nothing to offer but their votes. Insofar as they want them, Democrats can get these votes by stoking racial resentment. Insofar as getting these votes would require even a modest check on corporate excess, Republicans simply don't seem to want them at all.

At least at the level of leadership, neither party is focused on pursuing policies that would materially improve the stature of the poorest Americans. This apathy of politicians toward the poor breeds apathy among the poor toward the political process. These people feel detached and disinterested, casting ballots at a rate significantly lower than the general population. Indeed, both in midterm and presidential elections, Americans earning less than $40,000 have more than a 20 percent deficit in turnout compared to Americans earning above $75,000.[39]

Poor people, the sort of people who ride DART, are chronically dissociated. They are tuned out. They have little idea what's going on in this country, and that incomprehension precludes them from formulating a self-interested outlook and approach to interface within the American system. They are not thinking long term. They are not even thinking medium term. Like an emaciated castaway, satiating their basic needs is always their top priority. Maslow's hierarchy is a stubborn thing. They are too busy to learn how the world works, and they're too ostracized to care. Many of these people have a vague sense that systems are working against them, and most of them feel a general antipathy toward authority and institutions, but they don't understand the social and economic machinations of the country with the granularity that would be necessary to become upwardly mobile.

Thus, they are left to their own inadvertent devices, talking about the tedium of life in places like the train cars and buses of DART, far beneath America's proverbial Davids and even farther beneath its Goliaths.

CHAPTER 12

Getting Screwed

PRISONERS IN VICTORIAN ENGLAND WERE subjected to a number of physically demanding, often pointless ordeals. The free labor that they could provide was sometimes directed toward productive ends like chopping wood or grinding grain into flour, but in other instances labor was seen by authorities as an end in itself. One of the most notable examples of punitive, non-productive labor was the crank machine, a wooden box filled with sand. Attached to the wooden box was a crankshaft that could be turned, causing an internal turbine to churn through the sand. This exercise intentionally accomplished nothing; it transformed manpower into friction between the turbine blades and the sand. Rotations of the crankshaft were tracked on a mechanical dial, and in some institutions, prisoners were forced to complete more than 10,000 turns a day, meaning they would have to rotate the turbine every few seconds for an entire eight hours. As an additional punishment for especially unfortunate inmates, a screw could be tightened to intensify the labor, which offers a plausible etymological theory for the term "screw" to describe a jailer and the phrase "getting screwed" for being put in difficult circumstances.

After spending a considerable amount of time on DART, I can't help but reflect on how apt a metaphor the crank machine is for the absurdities of late-stage capitalism that torment America's lower classes.

As belabored in previous chapters, many of the people who ride DART are vagabonds who are only using the transit structures and vehicles for shelter. Other riders are employed. They have actual jobs that they need to travel to, and, owing to their culturally abnormal inability to access a personal vehicle, they are forced to take transit.

Seeing as the types of jobs these people perform are almost always in food service, hospitality, or construction, many of them are identifiable by their clothing. Sometimes, as I would commute to my job, I would sit and wonder about theirs. I would sit and watch a man in a McDonald's polo and imagine what it would be like to spend the entire upcoming day tending to a deep fryer rather than sitting behind a desk. I would look at the lifeless expression on the man's face and remember how terrible it was to work in a restaurant during my youth. My stomach would sink and my feet would start to ache just thinking about it, and I was much younger than him. I was lucky to be doing something else. He was not so lucky. This man was in his late twenties, and he was on his way to work a job that many high schoolers would balk at.

Those who are lucky enough to balk at this type of work *should* balk at it. Not everyone is in a position to be discerning in their employment, but the more people that are, the better. These jobs are terrible, and they aren't only terrible because they are low paying and physically exhausting, although they are. These low-skilled service jobs are terrible because they don't contribute a positive product or service to society. They are not generative in any meaningful sense. They facilitate a commercial process that generates profit, but they do not improve human well-being. They do not make society better-off as a whole. Americans do not lead happier lives because of McDonald's. Fast food makes people miserable. Fast food wastes people's money and degrades their health. People who work at fast-food restaurants, therefore, are not doing productive work. They are not contributing to society, a reality that must make working the job seem grievously unjust to those with the self-awareness to realize it.

Much like the crank machine, these mindless, low-paying jobs are a black hole for human potential. People toil simply to turn the crank. And, in a way, their toiling is just as punitive as it would be if they were churning sand, at least insofar as neither endeavor is pursued for any good reason and neither is facilitated with the slightest regard for the interests of the laborer.

Why, then, do these jobs exist? Why, if all they do is cause drudgery and despair, are there still so many jobs to be filled and, indeed, so many people willing to fill them?

The jobs exist, and people fill them because the relationship makes sense for both parties in the current American economy. These jobs reflect a desirable exchange for both parties. Commercial enterprises across the country offer roles that can be filled for the federal minimum wage of $7.25 an hour, and many people in America are willing to work them because the alternative is a lower level of poverty. Because these jobs are repetitive and low-skilled, an overwhelming number of them could, in fact, be automated, but automation is not an attractive option to corporations when human sweat is such a cheap commodity. And so the work is done, not because it makes the world a better place and not because it requires a human touch, but because it is profitable when done by desperate, disorganized humans for subsistence wages.

The lowest-paying jobs in the United States are largely unproductive. The government should just pay people a monthly universal basic income (UBI) to either eliminate them or force them to become more tolerable and higher paying.

"Well, that would lead to a labor shortage!"

It baffles me how many otherwise intelligent people will let stuff like this come out of their mouths.

Labor shortages don't exist. They aren't real. There's no such thing as a shortage of labor.

Or, at least, to say that there is a shortage of labor is merely to offer an opinion about the existing balance of power between the people who work and the people who pay them. Labor shortages are not brute economic facts like inflation or GDP. There is no threshold of scarcity beyond which a labor shortage can definitively be said to exist.

To say that there is a shortage of labor is merely to make a normative claim about the relationship between laborers and employers. It is to make a normative claim about the price at which employers are cosmically entitled to labor. It is to assert that the supply curve must slide down the demand curve so that workers earn less money.

The irony is that the people whose economic sensibilities are the most vehemently laissez-faire tend also to be the people who are most indignant when even the slightest pressures are put on firms to do a better job of attracting employees.

Throughout the pandemic, there were intervals where low-paying businesses complained about not being able to find workers because so many people were accessing extended COVID benefits, and in some cases, these businesses had to shut down or reduce their hours. In many cases, however, vacancies were just filled by migrants.

Contrary to what many Americans believe, it isn't an embrace of communism or an outright rejection of capitalism to insist on an income floor—an income floor that would organically exist if this country's corporations were not allowed to import an endless supply of unskilled labor from the third world.

A library of books could be written about this problem alone, but in one recent report from *The New York Times*, Hannah Dreier does an exceptional job of shedding light on the countless migrant children, some as young as twelve years old, who work low-skilled jobs across the country.[40] Some of the passages are jarring:

> In 2021, Karla Campbell, a Nashville labor lawyer, helped a woman figure out how to transport the body of her fourteen-year-old grandson, who had been killed on a landscaping job, back to his village in Guatemala. It was the second child labor death she had handled that year.
>
> Charlene Irizarry, the human resources manager at Farm Fresh Foods, an Alabama meat plant that struggles to retain staff, recently realized she was interviewing a twelve-year-old for a job slicing chicken breasts into nuggets in a section of the factory kept at 40 degrees.
>
> Unaccompanied minors have had their legs torn off in factories and their spines shattered on construction sites, but most of these injuries go uncounted. The Labor Department tracks the deaths of foreign-born child workers but no longer makes them public.

The architects of the American economy are so averse to the notion of higher wages for Americans that they will literally import what are essentially child slaves from Central America. In turn, this ceaseless flooding of the labor market creates an economy where corporations can force people to do painful, pointless work for appallingly low wages.

Just like in the Victorian prison, whether or not the work actually needs to be undertaken is totally unrelated to whether or not the work is undertaken. If all of the fast-food locations in the country closed down tomorrow and all of their employees stayed home, America would not be any worse off.

The only consequence of such a closure would be that those companies' shareholders would cease to profit off of the misdirected labor of the employees, and the employees themselves would no longer need to go to work. The employees would become unemployed, and that transition would be considered by the people who run the economy as intrinsically adverse. And therein lies the great economic absurdity of America: the fetishization of employment and the demonization of unemployment.

American political economic elites are obsessed with the concept of employment, and their obsession has trickled down to shape public sentiment so that regular people believe there is something intrinsically good and necessary about exchanging labor for wages. All Americans care about employment, and it often seems like it's all they do care about. During political campaigns, candidates argue about who has the best plan to create jobs. In the midst of a crisis like the COVID pandemic, all they boast about is getting people back to work. They treat employment, per se, as if it is somehow responsible for economic flourishing and self-actualization.

Scranton's own Joe "Blue-Collar" Biden put out an ad in February 2021, as businesses were reopening, that really typifies the sort of outlook on employment I'm referring to. In the ad, Biden calls a Californian named Michele Voelkert to discuss her loss of employment.

JB: "How are you, Michele?"

MV: "Well, I wrote you because, you know, I was laid off in July, and it's just been a tough time as far as trying to find work."

JB: "Working is a part of who you are. Like my dad used to say, 'A job is about a lot more than a paycheck. It's about your dignity. It's about your respect. It's about your place in the community'.... I admire your sense of responsibility and your desire to work."

MV: "What I related to you was when you talked about your father and how he had felt like he lost his dignity when he lost his job, and I think more than an income is that feeling needed and having a place to go, so I can't tell you how appreciative I am that you called me. Can my daughter say hello to you?"

JB: "Of course!"

MV's Daughter: "Hi, Mr. President."

JB: "How are you?"

MV's Daughter: "I'm good. How are you?"

JB: "It's so nice to speak to you. You should be very, very proud of your mom. That's why I called when I read the letter. I admire her—her determination, her commitment. It's pretty impressive. And so are you. So are you."

MV: "Thank you!"

JB: "Keep the faith."

Now, this was a political ad, and it was obviously scripted, but the proposition made by Biden does reflect how elites want working people to view employment: as a central and animating aspect of life from which to derive a deep sense of purpose and meaning.

Overstating just how fraudulent or delusional this mentality is cannot easily be done. Nobody who has ever been forced to take a low-paying, blue-collar job has ever felt this way. Normal, working-class people hate their jobs because their jobs are often incredibly difficult and degrading. Normal, working-class people work their jobs because they need money to pay rent and because they need to put food on the table. In a functional society, normal, working-class people do not rely on jobs for meaning; they rely on family, friendships, community, art, music, and other pursuits that are more elevated, dignified, and essentially human.

To be sure, this instance on maintaining high employment is not a partisan issue. A November 2018 interview between right-wing megastars, Tucker Carlson and Ben Shapiro, covered the economic impacts of automation:

> "Would you be in favor of restrictions on the ability of trucking companies to use this technology to artificially maintain the number of jobs that are available in the trucking industry?" asks Shapiro.
>
> "Are you joking? In a second! In a second! In other words, if I were president, I would say to the Department of Transportation, 'We're not letting driverless trucks on the road. Why? Really simple: Driving for a living is the single most common job for high-school educated men in this country, in all fifty states.' By the way, that's the same group whose wages have gone down by 11 percent over the last thirty years. The social cost of eliminating their jobs in a five-year span, ten-year span, thirty-year span, is so high that it's not sustainable. Look, capitalism is the best economic system I can think of, but that doesn't mean it's a religion and that everything about it is good. There's no Nicene Creed of capitalism. What I care about is living in a country where decent people can live happy lives. So, no, are you joking? And I would maybe make up some pretext for public consumption about how they're dangerous and how the technology isn't quite finessed. But, no, the truth would be that I don't want to put 10 million men out of work, because then you're going to have 10 million dead families and the cascading effect of that will wreck your country."

Of course, the idea that America's truckers could find something more pro-social and humane to do does not occur to Carlson, nor does the idea that the economic benefits generated by automation could be redistributed. Like so many Americans, he is unable to imagine a world where formerly working-class people find meaning and fulfillment in anything other than employment.

Carlson's is a deranged mindset. How could working-class people find meaning and fulfillment in their jobs? The jobs they are forced to do are so terribly dull and so obviously pointless. Working-class Americans churn sand for the capitalized, and if they were not so desperate for money, not so unbearably trapped by the unrelenting bills and quotidian chores of life at the bottom, they would do something else.

The great English novelist E. A. Blair observed how in the 1920s, Parisian *plongeurs* (dishwashers) would become swept up and battered by economic toil and hardship, often needlessly. He observed how unnecessary their work is, and, as I think about all of the people riding DART to their pointless jobs, flipping burgers, washing cars, mowing lawns, or any number of other vain capitalistic exploits, I struggle to find incongruities between Blair's diagnosis of the working poor in his time and my own diagnosis of the riders of DART:

> FOR what they are worth, I want to give my opinions about the life of a Paris *plongeur*. When one comes to think of it, it is strange that thousands of people in a great modern city should spend their waking hours swabbing dishes in hot dens underground. The question I am raising is why this life goes on—what purpose it serves, and who wants it to continue, and why I am not taking the merely rebellious, *fainéant* attitude. I am trying to consider the social significance of a *plongeur's* life.
>
> I think one should start by saying that a *plongeur* is one of the slaves of the modern world. Not that there is any need to whine

over him, for he is better off than many manual workers, but still, he is no freer than if he were bought and sold. His work is servile and without art; he is paid just enough to keep him alive; his only holiday is the sack. He is cut off from marriage, or, if he marries, his wife must work too. Except by a lucky chance, he has no escape from this life, save into prison. At this moment there are men with university degrees scrubbing dishes in Paris for ten or fifteen hours a day.

One cannot say that it is mere idleness on their part, for an idle man cannot be a plongeur; they have simply been trapped by a routine which makes thought impossible. If plongeurs thought at all, they would long ago have formed a union and gone on strike for better treatment. But they do not think, because they have no leisure for it; their life has made slaves of them.

The question is, why does this slavery continue? People have a way of taking it for granted that all work is done for a sound purpose. They see somebody else doing a disagreeable job, and think that they have solved things by saying that the job is necessary. Coal-mining, for example, is hard work, but it is necessary—we must have coal. Working in the sewers is unpleasant, but somebody must work in the sewers. And similarly with a plongeur' s work. Some people must feed in restaurants, and so other people must swab dishes for eighty hours a week. It is the work of civilization, therefore unquestionable. This point is worth considering.

Is a plongeur' s work really necessary to civilization? We have a feeling that it must be 'honest' work, because it is hard and disagreeable, and we have made a sort of fetish of manual work.

We see a man cutting down a tree, and we make sure that he is filling a social need, just because he uses his muscles; it does not occur to us that he may only be cutting down a beautiful tree to make room for a hideous statue. I believe it is the same with a plongeur. He earns his bread in the sweat of his brow, but it does not follow that he is doing anything useful; he may be only supplying a luxury which, very often, is not a luxury.

As an example of what I mean by luxuries which are not luxuries, take an extreme case, such as one hardly sees in Europe. Take an Indian rickshaw puller, or a gharry pony. In any Far Eastern town there are rickshaw pullers by the hundred, black wretches weighing eight stone, clad in loin-cloths. Some of them are diseased; some of them are fifty years old. For miles on end they trot in the sun or rain, head down, dragging at the shafts, with the sweat dripping from their grey moustaches. When they go too slowly the passenger calls them *bahinchut*. They earn thirty or forty rupees a month, and cough their lungs out after a few years. The gharry ponies are gaunt, vicious things that have been sold cheap as having a few years' work left in them. Their master looks on the whip as a substitute for food. Their work expresses itself in a sort of equation—whip plus food equals energy; generally it is about sixty per cent whip and forty per cent food. Sometimes their necks are encircled by one vast sore, so that they drag all day on raw flesh. It is still possible to make them work, however; it is just a question of thrashing them so hard that the pain behind outweighs the pain in front. After a few years even the whip loses its virtue, and the pony goes to the knacker. These are instances of unnecessary work, for there is no real need for gharries and rickshaws; they only exist because Orientals consider it vulgar to walk. They are luxuries, and,

> as anyone who has ridden in them knows, very poor luxuries. They afford a small amount of convenience, which cannot possibly balance the suffering of the men and animals.

So many Americans, likewise, are slaves to provide poor luxuries, *luxuries which are not luxuries.*

In the coming years, a huge portion of the American workforce will be undercut by automation. Even if the minimum wage remains where it is today, technological advancements will eventually shift the economic calculus for firms to make employing humans far less viable. This brute economic reality will be as true for white-collar industries as it is for blue-collar industries, if not more so. Just as robotics systems have superseded the fallible hands that once tilled fields, loaded container ships, and manned production lines, artificial intelligence softwares are superseding the fallible minds responsible for every flavor of administrative, executive, and even artistic work. Open AI's GPT-4 is already scoring in the 88th percentile on the LSAT. It's scoring in the 89th percentile on the math section of the SAT. What will GPT-5 be able to do? 6? 7? 8? Perhaps a better question is, "What tasks will it not be absurd to have performed by humans by the time these future iterations are inevitably released?"

Our reaction to this process should not be that of the retrograde pundits and politicians: "How can we delay automation to preserve jobs?" But rather, " How can the transition be expedited?" The only humane perspective is to emancipate wage slaves as immediately as possible. We shouldn't mourn or fear the loss of their jobs.

The most obvious catalyst to achieve this emancipation is a universal basic income. If Americans were paid even a modest monthly sum like the $1,000 initially proposed by 2020 presidential candidate Andrew Yang, they would be far less dependent on the labor market, and they would in turn be free to direct their energy toward pursuits that are generative and pro-social, like domestic work, art, and philanthropy.

Without a UBI, it's difficult to imagine the working-class people I see on DART being able to survive on their own. Our economic system is becoming increasingly technical, and these people have basically no technical skills. Absent UBI, they will soon have nothing that corporations would procure in exchange for a livable wage. It's not that the unskilled are any less valuable as human beings but simply that they are not positioned to sustain themselves in a highly automated, highly financialized, and highly sclerotic economy where wealth and influence aggregate among the most elite echelons of society.

Tens of millions of Americans have jobs that are miserable and unproductive. These people are members of the precariat class—a type of citizen whose offering to the labor market is mechanical, not cerebral, and who is therefore vulnerable to the stratifying progression of a non-redistributive economy. If wealthy Americans were taxed more heavily to fund a universal basic income, wages would rise, and fewer people would be forced into menial drudgery—fewer Americans would be getting screwed.

Implementation of a UBI should not be expected any time soon. It's something that America desperately needs right now, but just like our obsession with cars and our indifference to the obesity crisis, our thoughtless veneration of employment is a deeply entrenched part of this nation's culture. Most people oppose UBI, and they oppose it because they have been indoctrinated to believe that work is virtuous, even if the work in question consists of poisoning other poor people with food-adjacent slop for a quarter of the average national wage.

Our economic axioms are so painfully and pathologically messed up.

CHAPTER 13

Getting Used to It

A DISFIGURED POSSUM CARCASS IS A disgusting thing to look at. Dallas is full of possums, and these strange, rat-like creatures often get horribly mutilated after wandering out into traffic. If you ever find yourself as a pedestrian in this city, there's a good chance you'll encounter one.

I almost tripped over the first possum carcass I saw. I was walking home from the train, absentmindedly scrolling through a Spotify playlist when I peripherally noticed something gra y that nearly interrupted my stride. I didn't step in it, providentially. What a fucking mess that would have been.

Here was a grotesquely maimed possum. Like a bad car accident, I couldn't help myself from looking at it. I must have stood there for two or three minutes. I had never seen anything so ugly.

It nauseated me at first: the way its eyes had exploded out of its skull and the way its entrails appeared to have been vomited out during the final moments of life. The thing looked satanic.

But the longer I stared, the less the body repulsed me. And after five or ten minutes of staring at it, the sight seemed just about as normal and unremarkable as any of the other sights that I could have fixed my attention on, like the mockingbirds sitting on the wires overhead, the sagging oak trees that lined the street, or the crooked garbage bins in front of the houses. After five or ten minutes, I got used to looking at it.

When I first arrived in Dallas, the car culture, obesity, and wage slavery all seemed very ugly. Jarringly so. They seemed to be the clear symptoms of an *Americosis*, a sort of pernicious, tripartite cultural disease. After spending a year in the city, I still recognize these problems and appreciate the immense harm they inflict on society, but witnessing their manifestations doesn't shock me like it used to. Seeing an empty train car or an eighteen-lane highway doesn't seem as crazy to me now as it once did. I have gotten used to everyone resembling a sphere. And the destitution of the working poor doesn't arrest me as it once did. I am still aware of how serious all of these problems are, but I have become accustomed to living in their midst alongside an indifferent population. Thus, these problems don't affect me as viscerally as they did during my initial days in Dallas.

Americosis is like the mangled possum. It's a lurid, ugly thing to behold at first. Yet after spending considerable time in its midst, staring down its ugly, lifeless face, it begins to seem less offensive. It begins to seem less appalling. Dallasites and, indeed, most Americans are not disturbed by their ugly condition because the condition has been so comprehensively ugly for such a long period of time. Exposure ameliorates perceived abjection.

And so the disease goes untreated. And people get used to the disease. It's all just normal.

ENDNOTES

1. https://etcinstitute.com/directionfinder2-0/dart-demographics-study/
2. http://chrp.org/wp-content/uploads/2019/01/PDC-presentation-web-version.pdf
3. https://isotp.metro.net/MetroRidership/IndexRail.aspx
4. https://dart.org/about/about-dart/dart-facts
5. https://dartorgcmsblob.dart.org/prod/docs/default-source/marketing/financialdocuments/financial-statements/fy2021comprehensiveannualfinancialreport.pdf
6. https://www.bts.gov/content/reports-violent-crime-property-crime-and-arrests-transit-mode
7. https://www.iihs.org/topics/fatality-statistics/detail/state-by-state#fatal-crash-totals
8. https://mobilitylab.org/2016/09/08/transit-10-times-safer-driving-makes-communities-safer-says-new-apta-report/#:~:text=Per%20billion%20passenger%2Dmiles%20traveled,per%20mile%20than%20car%20trips.
9. https://twitter.com/dallasnews/status/1352789901746593799
10. https://wagner.nyu.edu/files/faculty/publications/Pink%20Tax%20Survey%20Results_finaldraft4.pdf
11. https://fee.org/articles/freedom-and-the-car/
12. https://taxfoundation.org/oecd-gas-tax/

13. https://crashstats.nhtsa.dot.gov/Api/Public/ViewPublication/812013
14. Miller, Ted R et al., "Costs of Crashes to Government, United States, 2008." *Annals of advances in automotive medicine*. Association for the Advancement of Automotive Medicine. Annual Scientific Conference vol. 55 (2011): 347–55.
15. https://www.valuepenguin.com/auto-insurance/car-ownership-statistics https://www.census.gov/programs-surveys/acs
16. https://www.experian.com/blogs/ask-experian/research/top-cities-with-the-highest-average-auto-debt/
17. https://www.badcredit.org/how-to/600-credit-score-car-loans/
18. https://www.fico.com/blogs/average-us-fico-score-ticks-706
19. https://www.shessinglemag.com/post/dating-without-a-car-is-it-a-good-idea
20. https://www.bolde.com/never-date-guy-doesnt-have-car/#:~:text=If%20you%20live%20in%20a%20major%20city%20with,guy%20without%20one%20is%20a%20big%20no-no.%20
21. https://www.standardmedia.co.ke/evewoman/general/article/2001247909/why-dating-a-man-who-does-not-drive-is-a-turn-off
22. https://apps.who.int/gho/data/view.main.MHSUICIDEASDRv?lang=en
23. https://www.tpl.org/2022-city-park-facts; https://www.eea.europa.eu/data-and-maps/daviz/percentage-of-total-green-infrastructure/#tab-chart_1
24. https://www.pure.ed.ac.uk/ws/portalfiles/portal/28632369/Urban_green_spaces_and_health_review_evidence.pdf
25. Sallis JF and Spoon C, University of California, San Diego, Making the Case for Designing Active Cities, Active Living Research, Technical Report, February 12, 2015.

26. https://www.cdc.gov/obesity/about-obesity/why-it-matters.html#:~:text=Obesity%20costs%20the%20US%20healthcare%20system%20nearly%20%24173%20billion%20a%20year.
27. https://www.ncbi.nlm.nih.gov/pmc/articles/PMC5640019/#:~:text=In%20particular%2C%20obesity%20is%20associated,present%20at%20work%20(presenteeism).
28. https://strongnation.s3.amazonaws.com/documents/484/389765e0-2500-49a2-9a67-5c4a090a215b.pdf?1539616379&inline%3B%20filename=%22Unhealthy%20and%20Unprepared%20report.pdf%22
29. https://coronavirus.jhu.edu/data/mortality
30. https://www.bmj.com/content/372/bmj.n623
31. https://www.sciencedaily.com/releases/2016/01/160120091704.htm
32. https://www.reuters.com/article/us-health-coronavirus-obesity/obesity-a-driving-factor-in-covid-19-deaths-global-report-finds-idUSKBN2AW1X0
33. https://fns-prod.azureedge.us/sites/default/files/ops/SNAPFoodsTypicallyPurchased-Summary.pdf
34. https://www.inside.iastate.edu/article/2021/06/17/beverage
35. https://dodsoco.ogc.osd.mil/Portals/102/Documents/Conflicts/CY%202022%2025K%20FY2021.pdf?ver=5EasEYEyRKHG3Emq14tvbg%3D%3D
36. https://www.americanactionforum.org/research/primer-agriculture-subsidies-and-their-influence-on-the-composition-of-u-s-food-supply-and-consumption/#_edn6
37. Waters H, DeVol R. Weighing Down America: The Health and Economic Impact of Obesity. Milken Institute. 2016. https://assets1b.milkeninstitute.org/assets/Publication/ResearchReport/PDF/Weighing-Down-America-WEB.pdf

38. https://www.pewresearch.org/fact-tank/2017/05/17/5-facts-about-u-s-political-donations/
39. https://equitablegrowth.org/evidence-from-the-2020-election-shows-how-to-close-the-income-voting-divide/
40. https://www.nytimes.com/2023/02/25/us/unaccompanied-migrant-child-workers-exploitation.html